James C. Beal

Rules for the General Government and Discipline

Of Members of the Police Force of Queensland

James C. Beal

Rules for the General Government and Discipline
Of Members of the Police Force of Queensland

ISBN/EAN: 9783744642316

Printed in Europe, USA, Canada, Australia, Japan

Cover: Foto ©Suzi / pixelio.de

More available books at **www.hansebooks.com**

1869.

—

QUEENSLAND.

RULES

FOR THE

GENERAL GOVERNMENT AND DISCIPLINE

OF MEMBERS OF THE

OLICE FORCE OF QUEENSLAND.

BRISBANE:

BY AUTHORITY: JAMES C. BEAL, GOVERNMENT PRINTER, WILLIAM STREET.

ERRATUM.

For "Inspector," in clause 22, page 8, *read* "Sub-Inspector."

INDEX.

	Page.	Clause.
Absence of members of Force from district	18	91
Absence, leave of—See "Leave."		
Accounts, examination and payment of...	44	
Acts of Council, extracts from, will be prepared for the	{ 60	65
guidance of the Force	{ 32	180
Acting sergeant	30	168
Affidavit of service of summons, form of...	61	68
Allowance of clothing, &c.	47	268
for station	48	270
Ammunition, supply of	9	29
Applications for leave of absence...	7	13
Appointments of police	48	269
date of new, to appear on back of abstract ...	44	248
certificate of	8	22
any party appropriating, on leaving the service,		
to be prosecuted	9	24
loss of, or damage to	9	26
Apprehensions, duties of constables in effecting... ...	32	181, 182
parties making, to attend at trial as witnesses ...	42	235
power of constables in effecting	51	
Arms, to be used on ordinary and other duty	10	30
fire, when to be loaded and discharged	10	32
fire, of escorts, always to be loaded, and when		
to be used	35	198
care of, by constables	9	28
sergeants responsible that constables take proper		
care of...	30	166
ammunition, appointments, &c.	48	269
to be examined before paying the men	8	22
of sergeant or constable, when leaving the Force,		
how to be disposed of	9	27
not to be taken on leave of absence	7	14

	Page.	Clause.
Arms, when a constable may proceed to extremities in use of	64	
Arrest.—See "Apprehensions."		
Articles lost or damaged to be charged to members of Force	9	26
Authority for special payments	47	264
Bail, when to be taken, by whom, when to be refused...	{38	218
	39	220
Barracks, regulations respecting (see also "Station") ...	11	
Baton to be used in ordinary police duty	{10	30
	65	89
Beat, duties of constable on	31	177
Bench of magistrates.—See "Magistrates."		
Board to examine horses	{14	65
	15	66
Books to be kept by officers	25	133
at watchhouse	38	216
Candidates, where and when to apply	2	3
on what conditions engaged	2	4
Certificates of leave of absence	6	12
of appointments	8	22
loss of	9	25
Charge, receipt and entry of, in charge book	38	216
of obstructing police, &c., when to be refused ...	38	217
to be regularly entered	56	40
Cheques, when to be drawn	47	265
Cheque books	47	266
butts of	47	267
Cleaning arms, to be taught	9	28
Commissioner, approval of, necessary to leaves of	{6	8
absence, when	7	13
complaints to	7	17
requisitions to be forwarded direct to	{10	33
	46	261
to direct purchase of horses	14	65
position and general duties of	20	104
is the channel for all communications from the police to the Government, &c.	20	98
result of inquests, &c., to be reported to ...	62	74
to furnish the Government with quarterly and annual reports	20	105
reports, when to be forwarded direct to... ...	43	241

	Page.	Clause.
Commissioner's office head-quarters of Force	2	2
members of Force visiting Brisbane to report themselves at, &c.	18	90
Clerk, constable allowed as		
Clothing, constables	{ 8 / 47	23 / 268
Combinations, members of the Force joining in, liable to punishment	8	20
Communications, what, to pass through the Commissioner	20	98
Complaints to Commissioner, how to be made	7	17
to be forwarded by officers	7	18
may be accompanied by explanatory statements of officers	7	19
unfounded, party making. liable to punishment...	8	21
Conditions upon which candidates are admitted into the Force		
Confession of a prisoner, when admissible as evidence...	40	226
Constable, obedience the first duty of	30	169
nature of the position of	{ 30 / 50	169 / 4
oath to be taken by	4	
pay of, while detained at depôt as supernumerary	4	(10)
period for which sworn in...		(16)
to devote his whole time to Government service	18	89
to live wherever directed	4	(11)
always to appear in police dress, unless by permission to the contrary	4	(12)
promptly to obey orders	4	(13)
to conform himself to Regulations of the Force...	4	(14)
never to take any money or gratuity without permission	4	(15)
cannot leave the Force without giving three months' notice	4	(16)
not to marry without permission of Commissioner	4	(17)
if dismissed, is liable to loss of pay due to him...	5	(18)
may be discharged for unfitness	5	(19)
not to question or disobey an order, but may afterwards complain	5	(20)
when in uniform not to smoke in streets ...	5	(21)

	Page.	Clause.
Constable, offences of, to be entered in defaulter's sheet	48	272
on leaving the Force, where defaulter's sheet to be sent to	48	274
when dismissed, not allowed to re-enter the Force	20	103
leave of absence	6	11
uniform of	47	268
may be directed to supply himself with new clothing, when	8	23
taught the use and care of arms, by whom ...	9	28
ammunition supplied to	9	29
when firearms required	10	30
not to load or discharge firearms unless ordered	10	32
powers of, to arrest, enter houses, &c.	50	5
powers of, greater, in cases of felony than misdemeanors	51	11
powers of, to arrest parties likely to commit, or found in, or charged with, commission of felony, &c.	51 52	
powers of, of arrest under various circumstances	51 52	
when to interfere without making an arrest ...	52	17
when to arrest in cases of assault	55	32
should arrest on command of a magistrate ...	55	33
may arrest parties for assaulting or opposing him in the execution of his duty	55	34
may turn parties out of house at request of owner	55	35
to arrest loose, idle, and disorderly persons, creating a disturbance	56	37
may arrest party maliciously causing injury to property	56	38
how to execute warrant	56 57	41 42
may arrest on warrant although it may not be in his possession...	57	43
execution of search warrant by	57	44
when to arrest intoxicated persons in the street	57	46
when to arrest prostitutes	57	47
when to arrest mendicants	57	48
when to arrest in cases of indecency	58	49, 50
to arrest parties using threatening language in the public streets	58	54

	Page.	Clause.
Constable, to arrest parties found cruelly ill-treating any animal...	58	55
when to arrest for gambling	58	52
may arrest on charge of third person	52 / 58	19 / 56
to afford protection to Sheriff in execution of writs	60	64
how summonses to be served by	61	68
on finding body of deceased person where to cause it to be removed to	62	69
to remain in charge of body until inquest	62	73
when to proceed to extremities in use of arms	64	
to use baton on ordinary police duty	65	89
to obey magistrates when called upon in cases of riot	65	90
when offence not actually committed, to watch suspected party	52	18
power of, to search boxes of persons charged with felony	53	22
to prevent as much as possible frauds on the revenue	53	23
duty of, with respect to persons carrying goods at night under suspicious circumstances, or loitering, &c.	53	24, 25
to be exercised in drill	11	39
under what conditions may leave barracks	12	46
leaving Force, penalty for taking clothing or appointments	9	24
to make himself acquainted with his beat	31	175
at a station not to follow any trade	12	50
to assist in providing station with wood and water when necessary	13 / 45	59 / 253
hours to be observed by	12 / 13	52, 53
not to be mounted or dismounted without the authority of the Commissioner	15	69
not to incur debts to publicans and others	31	173
to account for arms, &c., on leaving the Force	24	125
to make himself acquainted with his powers by law	32 / 50	180 / 6
to make himself acquainted with inhabitants, &c., in his neighborhood	31	176

	Page.	Clause.
Constable often required to act on his own responsibility	30	169
to execute lawful orders and commands of magistracy	{ 31	171
	{ 60	66
must be careful with regard to arms, appointments, clothing, horse, &c.	31	174
cannot be promoted unless he can write an official report or letter	31	172
extracts from Acts of Council to be prepared for instruction of... ... .,. ...	32	180
duties and responsibility of, when on beat ...	31	177
duties of, on apprehending any party	32	181, 182
not to search a prisoner by himself	32	183
to pay particular attention to public-houses, &c., and never to enter any, except on duty ...	33	185, 186
to report to sergeants anything causing danger or inconvenience in the streets	33	187
to give his name, number, &c., when called on to do so	33	188
to be civil and attentive to all classes	33	189
never to interfere unnecessarily, or with unnecessary violence	33	189
duty of, on a prisoner making a confession ...	40	226
principal duty of, to prevent crime	30	169
consequences of ill-treatment of horse by ...	15	68
not to use horse except on duty, nor in harness, except by order	16	76
to take care of horse, arms, accoutrements, &c., for which he is responsible	31	174
when he may break into a house...	{ 53	26
	{ 54	27
may require persons present to assist in making an arrest	54	28
may follow an escaped prisoner anywhere ; when may arrest for misdemeanor without warrant	54	30
duty of, in breaches of the peace	54	31
Contingencies	45	
Contracts for prisoners' rations, no person in Government employ to derive any advantage from		
Conveyance, vouchers to be certified	46	255
Correspondence, reports, &c., instructions respecting ...	43	

	Page.	Clause.
Correspondence, when to be forwarded to Commissioner through Inspector, and when direct ...	43	241
how to be written	43	242
of subordinate members of the Force to be written by themselves	43	243
dates, numbers, &c., of previous communications to be referred to	44	245
when received with a minute to be returned ...	44	245
letter not necessary to accompany the usual returns	44	246
when to be sent by despatch	43	239
generally to be forwarded from stations to head-quarters by patrols	43	240
Coroner, finding dead body to be reported to	62	71
in absence of, magistrate to hold magisterial inquiry	62	72
in what cases report to be made to ...	62	71
Crime, prevention of, principal duty of constables ...	51	12
Crime, reports of, what particulars they should contain	44	244
Criminal offence forms to be filled up and circulated ...	29	161
Cruelty to animals, arrest for	58	55
Death, violent or sudden, duties of police in cases of ...	62	
Debts to publicans, storekeepers, &c., not to be incurred by the police	31	173
Deceased constables, how effects to be disposed of ...	14	63
Defaulter's sheets to accompany the party on being transferred	48	272
who responsible for correctness of	48	273
where to be sent on party leaving the Force ...	48	274
Depôt, probation period of candidates to be passed at ...	3	(8)
Despatch duty, how to be performed	42	237
constables on, to be furnished with route ...	42	238
when communications to be sent by	43	239
Discharge, how arms to be disposed of, on	9	27
of constable, authority of Commissioner necessary to	24	128
Discharged constables not to sleep in police barracks ...	14	60
Dismissal liable to be followed by loss of pay	5	(18)
disqualifies from re-entering the Force	20	103
of sergeant or constable, on, how arms, &c., to be disposed of	9	27
of a constable, authority of Commissioner necessary to	24	128

	Page.	Clause.
Dismissed constable not to enter police barracks ...	14	61
District, transfer of, from one officer to another ...		
Districts, duties of members of Force in charge of ...	18	91
Disturbances, duties of police in cases of	55	36
Doors, when may be broken open by police	53	26
	54	27, 29
	55	36
Drill, necessity for	11	39
constable when engaged to be instructed at the depôt	4	(10)
officers to exercise their men in	11	40
Equipment of constables	48	269
Escorts, important and onerous part of police duty ...	33	190
course to be pursued by, on taking charge of prisoners or property	33	191
where to obtain accommodation during the night when necessary	34	194
not to allow prisoners to have intoxicating liquors	34	195
not to stop at public-houses during the day ...	35	196
to keep prisoners in centre of party	35	197
arms of, what necessary and when to be used ...	35	198
receipt and transport of property of prisoners under	35	200
duty of officers in charge of	36	201
how to return to their duty	36	204
to Judges or other Government officers, to be relieved at each station	36	205
when officers of the Force may be accompanied by	36	206
Felony, accusation of, how to be received at watchhouse	39	221
what offences are	51	8
when persons may be arrested for	51	13
boxes, &c., of person arrested for, may be searched	53	22
Fighting, duties of police in cases of	54	31
	55	36
Firearms, use of, by police	35	198
	64	
when to be loaded or discharged...	10	32
	35	198
Forage, requisitions for	10	35
	18	88
table of ration of, to be hung up at police station	16	75

	Page.	Clause.
Forage, when supply of, required notice to be given ...	17	82
course to be pursued on receipt of	17	83
to be used in order as supplied, old portion of stock first	17	85
by whom and to whom issued	17	84
storage of	18	86
allowance to constables	45	252
Formation of the Police Force	2	
Fuel and light	45	253
Furniture and repairs	47	262
Furniture, &c., register of, to be kept	20	101
Gambling, duties of police in cases of ..., ...	{ 58 } { 59 }	51 61
Good conduct, its influence on promotion		
Gratuity or money, &c., never to be received without permission	4	15
or gift, &c., not to be received by officers on promotion or removal	5	7
Handcuffs supplied to constables	⌈ 48 ⌊ 10	269 31
Head-quarters	2	2
Horses, when to be fed, watered, stabled, &c.	13	55
purchase of...	⌈ 15 ⌊ 16	65, 66
no advantage to accrue from, to any member of the Force	15	67
ill-treatment or neglect of...	15	68
registry of, where and by whom to be kept ...	15	70, 71
not in actual use, where to be kept	17	81
work to be fairly apportioned among	15	72
not to be kept clothed in stables unless sick ...	15	72
rate at which, should travel	16	73
when useless, how to be disposed of	16	74
parties having charge of, responsible that they have proper allowance of food	16	75
not to be used except on duty, nor in harness, except by permission	16	76
use of private, instead of Government	16	77
of men, not to be ridden by officers	16	78
not to be ridden by parties who are not members of the Force	17	78

	Page.	Clause.
Horses, when in bad condition, how to be treated ...	17	79
sales of, by public auction	17	80
supernumerary in a district	17	81
applications for additional	17	81
House, when may be broken into by police	53	26
	54	27
	54	29
	53	36
constable may direct a person to be turned out of, at request of owner	55	35
Impartiality and neutrality in political matters to be observed by members of the Force	2	
Indecency, duties of police in cases of	58	49, 50
Inquests or magisterial inquiries, duties of police in cases of	62	.
Inspector, responsibility of, with respect to accounts ...	23	123
nature of his duties generally	22	111
responsibility of, for the conduct of those under him	22	115
to make himself acquainted with the fitness of those under him for promotion	22	114
to be at all times ready to afford assistance in all matters connected with his duty	22	113
where to live, and not to leave district without permission of Commissioner	21	110
to visit stations, watchhouses, &c., in the district, and inspect books, as often as possible ...	22	117
to see that the men are acquainted with the use of their arms, their general duties, and the localities in which they are	23	118
to apportion duty among the men with impartiality	23	119
to see that proper system of patrols is established	23	120
to see that men under him do not fetter themselves in execution of their duty by incurring debts, &c.	23	121
to study economy in the expenditure of the Force	23	122
accounts, reports, &c., to be certified by, and regularly forwarded	23	123
duty of, on transfer of station or district from one officer to another...	23	124

	Page.	Clause.
Inspector, duty of, on receipt of order for the discharge or dismissal of any member of the Force ...	24	125
to give clear and precise instructions, and to report neglect to Commissioner	22	116
to send defaulters' sheet and registry with any sergeant or constable, on being transferred from one district to another...	24	126
when absent from head-quarters, or the district, who to act in his place	24	127
to report complaints	24	128
what complaints may be settled by, and when case to be referred to head of department ...	19	96
when to take constable misconducting himself before the bench, and decision thereof to be reported	24	128
complaints to, preferred by the public against the police	19	96
powers of, to punish members of the Force ...	19	96
may suspend from duty, but not dismiss or discharge any member of the Force without authority	24	128
to make himself acquainted with district ...	22	112
to be prompt in forwarding information of outrages or disturbances...	25	130
to see that the men exert themselves in the detection of crime	25	131
duty of, with respect to police benches	25 / 19	132 / 94
books and returns to be kept by	25	133, 134
when allowed services of sergeant or constable as clerk	26	137
not to innovate on the standing orders of the Force, but to communicate with the Commissioner when alterations may appear necessary	26	138
Intoxication in public streets, duties of police in cases of	57	46
on part of soldiers, &c., how to be treated ...	59	57
Introduction	1	
Judge, escort accompanying, to be relieved at each station...	36	205
Leave of absence, officers to report return from... ...	6	8

	Page.	Clause.
Leave of absence, officers applying for, to submit name of substitutes	6	9
renewal and extension of	6	10
how granted to sergeants and constables	6	11
for what period may be granted by officers in charge of districts	6	12
certificate of	6	12
when Commissioner's approval necessary to	7	13
parties on, not to take Government property with them	7	14
parties on, to whom to report themselves	7	14
in applying for, particulars of previous leaves to be given	7	15
parties on, subject to Rules and Regulations of the Force	7	16
misconduct while on, to be reported	7	16
in ordinary cases of sickness	49	276
Letters and despatches, conveyance of	42	237
Light	45	253
Magistrates, duties of police with respect to	19	94, 95
bench of, members of the Force may be tried by	19	96
bench of, remand of prisoners from one to another	29	158
power of, to direct arrest of any party	55	33
empowered to call for attendance of police	60	67
not vested with powers of interference with executive arrangements	60	67
in absence of coroner, to hold Magisterial inquiry	62	72
Marriage, permission of Commissioner necessssry to	4	(17)
Medical attendants on police, payment for	46	257
examination, candidates to undergo	3	(2)
without having first reported himself	48	275
certificate required in all cases of sickness	49	278
Members of Force, to devote whole time to the service	18	89
on duty or leave in Brisbane, to report at Commissioner's office	18	90
absent from district or station duties, devolve on next in rank	18	91
in charge of station, district division responsible	18 / 19	92 / 93

	Page.	Clause.
Members of Force to act in accordance with wishes of the Bench	19	94
to pay strict and prompt obedience to order of magistrates	19	95
offences committed by, how tried	19	96
to attend at police court	19	97
presumed to know their duty	20	99
to keep register of Government property ...	20	101
engaged for one year, &c....	20	102
Mendicants, duties of police with regard to	57	48
Minute, communication when received with, to be returned	44	245
Misdemeanor, accusation of, how to be received at watchhouse	39	221
Mounted constable.—See "Constable."		
Murder, duties of police in cases of	62	75
Night allowance	45	250
when not granted	45	251
Neglect of duty to be reported ... ... `	20	100
Notice required before leaving the Force	4	(16)
Nuisances to be reported by constables	60	62
Oath to be taken by police constables	4	(9)
Occurrence book, officer issuing pay to make certain entries in	8	22
state of stations to be entered in,when and by whom	22	117
Offences of sergeants and constables to be entered in defaulters' sheet	48	272
of members of the Force on leave to be reported	7	16
of police against the public, treatment for ...	19	96
felonies, misdemeanors	51	7,8, 9, 10
when not actually committed constable to watch suspected person	52	18
to be reported by constables	59 / 60	60, 61 62, 63
Officers not to receive gifts, gratuities, &c., from the men, on promotion or removal	5	7
receipt of gratuities, &c., from the public by ...	5	7
not to absent themselves from station or district without permission	6	8

	Page.	Clause.
Officers, applications for leave of absence by	6	9
by what, leaves of absence may be granted ...	6	12
to forward complaints to Commissioner	7	18
may direct a constable to supply himself with new clothing	8	23
signing requisitions for articles not required to pay amount	10	36
only to sign requisitions	11	38
occasionally to exercise men in drill	11	39
responsible for state of stations, arms, &c., under their charge	11	41
to keep registry of horses...	15	70
not to use horses except on duty, nor in harness except by permission...	16	77
applications of, to be allowed to use private horses	16	77
not to ride horses of men under their command	16	78
in referring to previous communications, to give date, number, &c.	44	245
not to forward despatches by mounted men ...	43	239
in charge of districts responsible for accuracy of defaulters' sheets	48	273
in charge of districts fairly to apportion work among men and horses	15	72
in charge of stations not to follow any trade ...	12	50
in charge of stations to attend stable parade ...	13	56
in charge of escorts, where to march	36	201
in commission of peace not expected to take bench duty	2	
in charge of stations to get up cases for coroner	62	71
Orderly, no officer of the Force to be accompanied by ...	36	206
Orders, how to be received and executed	4	(13)
not to be questioned	5	(20)
improper, members of the Force have a right to complain of	5	(20)
Patrols, establishment of	37	207
to be established by Inspectors	37	207
to be formed by return escorts	36	204
particulars of, to be entered in occurrence book...	37	208
how duty of, should be performed	37	209
times at which, to go out, places to visit ...	37	210
to apprehend disorderly and suspicious persons met at unseasonable hours	38	212

	Page.	Clause.
Patrols, constables on, not to separate, talk, smoke, or enter public-houses	38	214
Paupers, burial of	46	258, 259
Pay abstracts, when to be forwarded	45	249
Payment of the Force	44	247
Police, different ranks of	2	1
candidates for, when and where to apply ...	2	3
conditions on which candidates admitted into ...	2	4
notice required before leaving	4	(16)
Police magistrates, lawful orders to be obeyed by police	19	95
cases to be tried by	19	96
duties of, appointed to act as Inspectors ...	21	
Politics, impartiality and neutrality in, to be observed	2	
Printed forms	48	271
Prisoners apprehended for felony, boxes of, may be searched	53	22
escaped, may be followed into any place ...	53	26
treatment of, after arrest	56	39, 40
in custody of constable till discharge, committal, or conviction	56	40
remand of, duty of officers on	29	158
when to be searched, and by whom	32 / 36 / 40	183 / 202 / 225
when and by whom to be admitted to bail ...	38 / 39	218 / 220
confession of, when admissible as evidence ...	40	226
provisions and refreshments for	41	227, 230
to be frequently visited, and if ill to be attended to	41	231
under escort, security of, first consideration ...	33	191
precaution to be taken in the escort of	33	191
under escort, meals supplied to	34	194
under escort not to be allowed intoxicating liquors	34	195
under escort to be kept in centre of party ...	35	197
under escort, when they may be fired at ...	35	199
under escort not to be left in possession of property	35	200
under escort to be searched before taken charge of	36	202

	Page.	Clause.
Prisoners under escort, warrants for, to be examined ...	36	202
treatment of, after arrest	32	182, 183
Promotions made from next inferior rank	5	5
principal things considered in	5	6
applications for, how to be made	5	7
chance of, open to every member of Force ...	5	5
to rank of sergeant, not made unless party can write a good official letter or report ...	31	172
Property in possession of police, disposal of	29	159
charge and transfer of, at police stations ...	11 / 23 / 20	43 / 124 / 101
in what manner to be taken from prisoners ...	32	183
receipt and disposal of, at watchhouses	32	183
under escort, security of, first consideration ...	33	191
precautions to be taken in escorting	34	192
of Government, charge of, at police stations ...	11	43
of prisoners, disposal of	29	159
of prisoners under escort, care of	35	200
Prosecutors, duties of the police as	41	232
Prostitutes wandering in the streets, &c.	57	47
Public-houses, duties of police respecting	33 / 59 / 62	185 / 61 / 69
Punishments, power to inflict, possessed by officers in charge of districts	19	96
Quarters, responsibility for state of	11	41
of sergeants and men to be visited by Sub-Inspector	27	145
See also under "Station."		
Questions to be answered by candidate for Force ...	3	(9)
Ranks, different, in the Force	2	1
Register of horses, by whom to be kept...	15	70
to accompany sergeants or constables on being transferred	24	126
Remand of prisoners from one bench to another ...	29	158
Report, annual and quarterly, to be furnished to Government by Commissioner	20	105
to be made to the Commissioner in cases of wounds or injuries received in the performance of his duty	49	277

	Page.	Clause.
Reports, instructions respecting.—See "Correspondence."		
Requisitions, to whom to be forwarded	10	33
how to be made out	10	34
for forage, conveyance of constables or prisoners, &c.	10	35
to whom to be presented for payment	10	36
if given for articles not actually required, who responsible	10	36
counterfoil of book to be preserved	10	37
by whom may be signed	11	38
for clothing, stationery, and stores	46	261
Resignation, notice of	29	160
Returns, to be kept by officers or sergeants in charge ...	25	134
to be kept by Sub-Inspectors	25	133
usual, in forwarding, no letter required	44	246
Revenue, fraud on, to be prevented	53	23
Riot, conduct of police in cases of	54	31
Route to accompany a constable when on despatch duty	42	238
Seniority not the principal consideration in promotions	5	6
Sergeant, duties of, those of acting Sub-Inspector ...	29	162
duty of	29	162, 163
to inspect men going on and coming off duty ...	30	167
to be impartial and take his regular tour of duty	29	163
responsible for appearance of men, their arms, &c.	30	166
acting	30	168
when in charge of station to keep same books as Sub-Inspector	26	135
Sheriff to be assisted by police	60	64
Smoking, constables in uniform not to indulge in, in public places	5	(21)
Soldiers, intoxication of	59	57
Stable parade, hours of	13	54
to be attended by officer in charge of station ...	13	56
Station, parties in charge of, responsible	11, 18, 19	41, 91, 92
who responsible for damage	11	42
list of articles in each room of, to be hung up ...	11	43
transfer of charge of	11	43
absence of constables from, to be noted	12	44, 45

	Page.	Clause.
Station, under what conditions may be left by constable, how many, &c.	12	46
poultry, &c., not to be kept at	12	48
to be kept clean	12	49
officer in charge of, or constable at, not to follow any trade	12	50
hours to be observed at	12	52, 53
fires to be allowed in, supply of wood and water to	13	58, 59
officer in charge of, to attend stable parade	13	56
persons unconnected with, not to sleep in	14	60
to be inspected by Inspector	22	117
Stolen goods, disposal of	57	44
Streets, danger or inconvenience in, to be reported by constables	33	187
Sub-Inspector, in absence of Inspector, to represent that officer	27	147
responsible for drill of men	27	141
to keep roster of duties performed	27	142
to inspect horses	27	144
to inspect quarters of sergeants and men, and when	27	145
his position, a somewhat confidential one	27	146
not to leave district without permission	28	150
responsible for conduct, &c., of constables	26	140
responsible for state of barracks, arms, &c.	26 / 28	140 / 152
to attend daily at Inspector's office with reports	27	143
to inspect men, horses, arms, &c., on going on duty, and on return from	27	144
in absence of, Inspector to act	27	147
to make himself acquainted with roads, passes, and bush generally, in the neighborhood of station	28	153
to divide duty equitably among the men	28	151
demeanor of	27	149
to make himself acquainted with public-houses, &c., in his division	28	157, 155
course to be pursued by, on remand of prisoners	29	158
duty respecting the disposal of property	29	159

	Page.	Clause.
Sub-Inspector to report all matters connected with the peace of his locality	28	154
to forward resignations, correspondence, &c., intended for the Commissioner's office to Inspector	29	160
to circulate notices of criminal offences	29	161
books and returns to be kept by	2S	15G
Suicide, cases of	62	74
Summonses	60	66, 68
Supernumerary constable at depôt, pay of	4	(10)
Suspension from duty	24	128
Testimonials to be produced by candidates	3	(4)
Testimony, how it should be given by police	41	232
prevarication or partiality in, to be punished ...	42	234
person who cannot give, properly, unfit for the Force	42	234
Unfitness, constable may be discharged for	5	(19)
Uniform, members of the Force to appear in	4	(12)
Uniform	47	268
Veterinary surgeon	14	65
Violence, unnecessary, constables warned against ...	33	189
Vouchers to be accompanied by letter of advice ...	47	263
Warrant necessary for the detention of prisoners after having once been before a magistrate ...	38	219
prisoner apprehended on, by whom to be admitted to bail...	39	220
for prisoner under arrest to be examined before prisoner is taking charge of...	36	202
should generally be obtained before breaking into a house	54	27
generally necessaay before arresting for misdemeanors	54	30
how to be executed	56	41
search	57	44
to be executed by order of magistrates	60	66
Watchhouse, prisoners to be searched at		
constable always on duty at	38	215
receipt and entry of charges at	⎰38	216
	⎱56	40
when charge of obstructing a constable in execution of his duty to be refused at	38	217

XX.

INDEX.

XX.

INDEX.

XX.

INDEX.

XX.

INDEX.

XX.   INDEX.

	Page.	Clause.
Watchhouse, bail, when and by whom to be taken at, and when refused	38	218
prisoner not to be detained in, without warrant, after having been once before a magistrate...	38	219
charges of felony or misdemeanor, how to be received at	39	221
property brought to constables in charge of, to be entered, &c.	40	224
confession from prisoner in custody at, when admissible as evidence	40	226
provisions allowed by Government, and refreshments to prisoners at	41	227, 230
keeper responsible for search	40	225
fuel and light	45	253
wood for, when to be provided by police ...	45	253
supplies, vouchers for	45	254
Whistle, when to sound	32	179
Witnesses, duties of the police as	41	232
parties making arrest to attend at trial as ...	42	235
in civil cases, expenses of constables as, by whom to be paid	42	236

RULES

FOR THE

GENERAL GOVERNMENT AND DISCIPLINE

OF MEMBERS OF THE

POLICE FORCE OF QUEENSLAND.

———◆———

Colonial Secretary's Office,
Brisbane, 12th May, 1869.

HIS Excellency the Governor, with the advice of the Executive Council, has been pleased to cancel all existing Rules for the general government and discipline of Members of the Police Force, and to approve and confirm the following Rules, which are hereby published in the *Government Gazette*, in terms of the seventh section of the Act 27 Victoria, No. 11.

By His Excellency's Command,
ARTHUR HODGSON.

———

INTRODUCTION.

THE following revised Rules for the Police Force have been established by His Excellency the Governor in Council, under the provisions of the Act 27 Victoria, No. 11, in order that it may be conducted upon one uniform system, and that its members may not be embarrassed in the execution of their several duties from the want of proper instructions.

Officers of Police who are in the Commission of the Peace, are, as a general rule, not expected to take Bench duty. If at any time they are at or near a Court of Petty Sessions, when from the absence of Magistrates, or a deficiency in the number required by law to act, their sitting in Court would be advantageous to the interests of the public, they may act judicially, provided their executive Police duties are not thereby interfered with. They are not, however, to act in any case where a member of the Police Force is either complainant or defendant.

Both officers and men are studiously to observe neutrality in political matters.

FORMATION.

1. The Police Force of Queensland consists of the following ranks, viz.:—

Commissioner
Inspectors } Officers.
Sub-Inspectors
Sergeants
Constables.

2. The head-quarters of the whole Force shall be in Brisbane, under the immediate supervision of the Commissioner of Police.

3. All candidates for admission into the Police Force are to attend, with an application in their own handwriting, and such testimonials as they may have, at the Commissioner's office, at ten a.m. on any Wednesday. No candidate need, under any circumstances, apply elsewhere.

CONDITIONS.

4. The conditions under which candidates are admitted into the Police Force are stated here, that no complaint may be made hereafter, upon their being enforced; but the Commissioner has the power, subject to the approval of His Excellency the Governor in Council, to alter or annul any of these conditions, and also to make such new rules as may be found expedient.

(1.) Candidates to be eligible for the Force must be under the age of thirty, unless they have previously been engaged in police duty, in which case they may be admitted up to the age of thirty-five.

(2.) As they have to undergo a medical examination, they must be of a strong constitution, and free from any bodily complaint.

(3.) They must be able to read and write well.

(4.) They must produce satisfactory testimonials of character, either from those under whom they have served at home or from parties of respectability in the colony.

(5.) The candidates are to understand, that in engaging for service in the Police Force, it is not only for police duties, but for fatigue or any other work they may be ordered to perform by their superior officers.

(6.) They will be taken on for general police service, and those who are best adapted will be selected for mounted duty, but are liable at any time, on its being considered advisable, to be dismounted.

(7.) They will be taken on in the first instance for not less than three days on trial, without pay, but before enrolment they must be certified to by the medical officer appointed for the purpose, as being physically fit for the service.

(8.) During the period of probation, which is always passed at the depôt, they can leave at any time, by giving notice to the officer in charge.

(9.) After the period of probation, they are, if considered suitable, required to fill up in their own handwriting answers to the following queries, attaching their signature thereto, and to take and subscribe, in the presence of a magistrate, the following oath, as required by the Act 27 Victoria, No. 11.

QUESTIONS.

Have you been in any police or public service; if so, in each case, state what and where?

For what time?

When discharged, and why?

By whom last employed, and where?

By whom recommended?

Married or single?

Signature :

OATH.

I,   do swear that I will well and truly serve our Sovereign Lady the Queen in the office of constable, without favor or affection, malice or ill-will, for the period of one year from this date, and until I am legally discharged ; that I will see and cause Her Majesty's peace to be kept and preserved, and that I will prevent, to the best of my power, all offences against the same; and that while I shall continue to hold the said office I will, to the best of my skill and knowledge, discharge all the duties thereof faithfully, according to law—So help me God.

(10.) In order that all newly appointed constables may have an opportunity of acquiring a knowledge of drill, and the more simple duties of the service, a certain number of supernumeraries will always be maintained at the depôt, for the purpose of supplying such vacancies as may occur in the various divisions ; and during the period they are retained on the list of supernumeraries, they will receive but three shillings per diem.

(11.) They are to serve and reside wherever they may be ordered, and shall be ready at all times to move in any direction that may be found necessary.

(12.) They are to appear in the police dress at all times, unless leave be given to the contrary.

(13.) They are promptly to obey all lawful orders which they may receive from the persons placed in authority over them.

(14.) They are to conform themselves to all the regulations which may be made from time to time for the good of the service.

(15.) They are not, upon any occasion, or under any pretence whatever, to take money or any gratuity from any person without the express permission of the Commissioner.

(16). Persons appointed to the Force are sworn in for one year in the first instance, during which period they cannot voluntarily leave the Force ; but when they have served a year they can leave after having given three months' notice.

(17.) No man in the Police force shall marry without permission from the Commissioner.

(18.) If he be dismissed the Police Force, the whole of his pay then due or unpaid is liable to be forfeited.

(19.) Any constable is liable to be discharged for unfitness, or dismissed for negligence or misconduct, independently of any other punishment to which he may by law be subject.

(20.) Any constable who questions or disobeys the orders he may receive from a superior officer will be severely punished ; every officer or sergeant in charge is held strictly responsible that he immediately reports any individual who refuses to obey him in any matter of duty. At the same time, the men are informed, (although obedience is their first and most especial duty) that they have a right respectfully to complain of any officer from whom they may receive any improper orders..

(21.) Police constables in uniform, whether on duty or not, are prohibited from smoking in the streets or public places.

PROMOTIONS.

5. All vacancies in the rank above that of constable will, as far as may be practicable, be filled up by promotion from the next inferior rank ; every inducement is thus held out for men of a good class to enter the Force, and to exert themselves while in it ; for by zealously and efficiently performing their duties to the public they will be consulting their own interests.

6. At the same time it must be understood, that seniority, length of service, and good conduct are not of themselves the main recommendation for promotion ; for although they will always have their due weight, efficiency and adaptation for the particular vacancy will be the principal considerations. Hence those desirous of promotion must endeavour to merit it by a zealous attention to their duties, and the favorable report of their immediate superior officer will be an indispensable requisite for advancement to superior grades.

7. No member is to make application for promotion except through the usual official channels ; and no officer is to receive any gift, address, or other token of respect or approval, on his promotion or change of jurisdiction,

from the men who have served or are serving under him ; for if the subordinate ranks of the service are permitted to express their approval of the conduct of their superiors, they might also assume it as a right to condemn it ; and as the expression of either praise or censure would be alike opposed to all discipline and good order, they are both equally and strictly forbidden. Nor can any officer be allowed to receive any such present, address, or token of respect from the public, except with the sanction of the Commissioner of Police.

LEAVE OF ABSENCE.

8. No officer is to absent himself from his district or station except on duty, without permission from the Commissioner. Every officer who shall obtain leave of absence is to return to his quarters on the evening of the day on which the period of such leave shall terminate, and is to report his return accordingly on the following day in the usual manner to the Commissioner.

9. When an officer applies for leave of absence, he is to submit the name of the member of the Force who is to act for him, and such member of the Force will be held responsible for the correct discharge of that officer's duties during his absence.

10. Leave of absence granted to an officer of the Force will not be renewed or extended, except in case of urgent necessity, which must be clearly shown by the officer applying for such extension, and in the event of illness being the plea for an extension of leave, a medical certificate of such illness must accompany the application.

11. When Sub-Inspectors, Sergeants, and constables are allowed leave of absence, it will be according to the following scale :—

For any period not exceeding seven days, on full pay ; above seven, and not exceeding fourteen days, on half-pay ; and for any period exceeding fourteen days, without pay.

12. Officers in charge of districts may occasionally grant leave of absence for periods not exceeding three days, but not beyond the boundary of their respective

districts; and in every case they will give to the party obtaining leave a certificate of the fact, on one of the printed forms supplied for the purpose, carefully preserving the counterfoil for reference.

13. Applications for leave of absence for more than three days must, in every case be submitted for the approval of the Commissioner.

14. Men going on leave are not to take any part of their arms or appointments, or any Government horse with them, and are to report themselves to the senior officer of the Force at or near whose station they may be residing while on leave.

15. In all applications for leave of absence, it must be stated at what periods, and for what length of time, the applicant had been absent during the year previous to the date of application.

16. Members of the Force when on leave are to consider themselves subject to every order, rule, and regulation of the Force, and as liable to be called on to act as constables, and to the consequences of any breach of discipline or good order, as if they were serving at their proper stations; and all members of the Force, whether officers or otherwise, are required to report all cases of misconduct, on the part of men on leave of absence, whether such misconduct may have been witnessed by them or reported to them by others.

COMPLAINTS.

17. Members of the Police Force can at any time make any representations they may wish to the Commissioner; all that is required being, that the complaint shall be in writing, and that it shall be made in a respectful manner, and forwarded through their immediate superiors.

18. Any officer on receiving any complaint will forward it to the officer in charge of the district, who, if it be intended for the Commissioner, will forward it accordingly.

19. While the officers are to consider it imperative upon them to forward all such complaints, they should accompany them by such statements of their own, bearing

reference to the subject of the complaint, as they may consider necessary.

20. Every attention that justice, reason, and expediency admit, will be paid to the wants or wishes of the constables ; but all combinations, and, as a general rule, any petition signed by numbers, for any purpose, will subject those who sign it, or join such combination, to punishment.

21. The means of redress are at all times open to any member of the Force who may think himself aggrieved ; but it is to be understood that protection will be equally afforded to any person against whom frivolous or unfounded complaints may be made; and the person making such, more especially when against his own superiors, will himself be liable to a proportionate punishment.

ARMS, AMMUNITION, APPOINTMENTS, Etc.

22. Each Member of the Force below the rank of Inspector will be furnished, at the expense of the Government, with clothing, arms, ammunition, appointments, &c. On being supplied with these, or such other articles as it may be deemed advisable to supply him with, he will be required to sign a certificate containing a list of them, the date of issue, statement of condition when issued, together with any other remarks it may be necessary to insert, which certificate will be countersigned by the officer issuing the articles, and must be retained by the party supplied and be produced prior to his receiving his monthly pay; and the officer by whom the pay is issued, after examining the articles, will enter in the Station Occurrence Book a certificate to the following effect :—

I certify that on paying the men of this station, I carefully examined all the articles mentioned in their certificates, and find that they were all in good and serviceable order.

23. Whenever any constable's dress shall be observed to be in an improper state, the officer under whom he is. serving, if above the rank of Sub-Inspector, shall have the power to order him to.be supplied with whatever article he may require, and the cost of such, although supplied against the wish of the constable, will be deduc-

ted from his pay ; the whole proceeding being, of course, subject to the approval of the Commissioner.

24. In the event of any member of the Force, on leaving the service, taking with him any of the articles mentioned in the certificate, he will be prosecuted for felony,

25. Any one losing or defacing the certificate will be charged two shillings for a new one, and it will be presumed that he had been provided with every article mentioned in it.

26. In case of any of the articles being lost or damaged through intention or neglect of any member of the Force, the amount of the cost of the articles lost, or the damage, will be charged against him in proportion to the original cost ; and the amount must be forwarded direct to the Commissioner, by whom it must be received before the other articles can be supplied.

27. When any Sub-Inspector, sergeant, or constable receives his discharge, or is dismissed from the Police Force, the officer in charge of the district will see that his clothing, arms, accoutrements, or any other Government property in his possession, are returned to store in a clean and proper state, and not used till his successor is appointed ; and should state on the back of his parchment certificate in what condition the arms, &c., issued to him were returned, and should forward the certificate to the Commissioner's office, from whence a new one will be supplied for his successor, without which the kit must not be issued.

28. Each man will be taught by the sergeant or officer, under whose immediate charge he is placed, the proper manner of cleaning and keeping his arms, &c., in good order.

29. He will be supplied with twenty rounds of ammunition, and in the event of the quantity being unaccounted for at any time, the amount of sixpence for every missing cartridge will be deducted from his pay ; when applying for more, he will state in writing how and what that previously issued had been expended.

30. On ordinary police duty, the baton, with the addition of a pistol, when it is probable firearms will be required, need only be carried, except on prisoner or gold escort.

31. A certain number of handcuffs will be supplied to each watch-house keeper, for which he will be responsible.

32. No constable is to presume to load or discharge his firearms, unless ordered to do so by his superior officer, or in cases of emergency.

REQUISITIONS.

33. All requisitions for supplies must be sent direct to the Commissioner.

34. In every case, requisitions must be signed by the officer or sergeant in charge of the station where the supplies are required, and countersigned by the officer in charge of the district; and no requisition whatever will be attended to unless it contains particulars of former supply, how disposed of, and the quantity and condition of stock on hand.

35. For the purpose of providing for the supply of forage to mounted constables, when at a distance from any police station, or procuring conveyance for constables or prisoners, or other services of the kind, a requisition book is given to each officer of the Force, who, in the case of any supplies or services of this nature being required, will fill up one of the forms, and give it to the party making the supply or performing the service.

36. Every such requisition, signed by an officer of police, should be forwarded by the party to whom payment is to be made, with the usual voucher in duplicate to the officer in charge of the district; but should it appear that a requisition has been given for any supply that was not required for the public service, or for any supplies for constable, such as meals, beds, &c,, which should be borne by the usual sum allowed them as night allowance, the amount will be deducted from the pay of the officer signing the requisition.

37. In all cases wherein these requisitions are given, the full particulars must be entered in the counterfoil

of the book, which must be carefully preserved for reference.

38. All members of the force below the rank of Sub-Inspector are strictly forbidden to sign these requisitions, as the Government do not hold themselves responsible for articles so obtained.

DRILL.

39. All officers, whether in charge of districts or stations, will take occasional opportunities to exercise their men in the manual and platoon movements: but it is to be understood that such exercises are not in any way to interfere with the discharge of their regular police duties.

40. The principal object to be kept in view, in all exercises in drill and the use of arms, is to make the force effective, and not to make it approximate in its character to a military body, further than by introducing the promptness and uniformity of action attained in such bodies.

BARRACKS, STABLES, Etc.

41. The officer in charge of a station will be held strictly responsible for the state of his quarters, which must always be orderly, cleanly, and fit for inspection ; the arms, accoutrements, clothing, and barrack furniture, being regularly arranged, and kept in good and serviceable repair and order.

42. All damages must be promptly reported to the officer in charge of the district; and when occurring through carelessness or negligence, the officer in charge at the time will be responsible that the cost of the repairs is defrayed by the person through whom the damage has occurred, and in the event of his failing to discover the offender, he will defray it himself.

43. A board, with a list of all articles the property of the Government, will be hung up in each room, and the officer, sergeant, or constable in charge of the station, will be held responsible for the articles mentioned therein ; and in the event of such officer, sergeant, or constable

being removed, the officer relieving him will take care that the articles correspond with the list, and are in serviceable condition ; if not, a report must be forwarded to the Inspector of the district.

44. If any man should report himself unable, from illness, to attend any parade or to perform any duty, the officer in charge is to note the circumstance in his occurrence book.

45. He is to make an immediate report of any man who absents himself from any parade or duty (unless illness be the cause of such absence), or from quarters at night, whether in barracks or not.

46. No man shall leave his barracks without acquainting the sergeant or constable on duty where he is to be found, nor go from his station any greater distance than a quarter of a mile, without permission from the party in charge ; men living out of barracks must not be absent from their quarters after ten p.m. without permission.

47. Except when on duty, no greater number than one-half the Force at a station shall leave their quarters, or their immediate vicinity.

48. No poultry, cows, horses, goats, pigs, or other animals, are to be kept by the police without permission.

49. The men are to keep every part of the barracks, its approaches, passages, and yards, clean and in good order, and are to study to uphold an appearance of neatness and regularity in everything connected with their post.

50. The officer in charge is not himself to follow any trade or business, nor suffer his men to do so, for his time, as well as theirs, and that of all the Force, belongs to the public, and must be wholly devoted to its service. The officer in charge will be held strictly responsible for the due observance of this regulation.

51. The windows must be kept clean, and should be opened whenever the weather will admit of it, and must be instantly repaired whenever they require it.

52. As regards hours, the following should, where practicable, be observed at all police stations in the colony :—All constables, with the exception of those who have been employed on night duty, should rise in the

morning not later than six, they should be dressed and their bedding neatly folded during the next half hour, and the rooms should be swept and set in order immediately afterwards.

53. The hour for breakfast should be eight a.m. ; for dinner, one p.m. ; and for tea or supper, six p.m. At half-past nine such men as have not leave, or are not on duty should go to bed, and all lights and fires, except such as are authorised to be kept up during the night, should be extinguished by ten o'clock.

54. Where the men are mounted, they should attend morning stable parade at six o'clock.

55. The horses should then be taken to water, and after returning should be properly groomed, and receive the regulated allowance of food ; this, when water is in the neighborhood, should not occupy more than one hour. At noon such horses as may not be on duty should be again watered and fed. The hour for evening stables should be five o'clock, when the horses should be again taken to water, and after returning be properly cleaned, fed, and bedded down for the night ; every man's saddle and bridle being properly cleaned and carefully placed away on the saddle rack.

56. The officer in charge of the station should always attend stable parade, to see that the men groom their horses properly.

57. From the great variety in the different police duties, it cannot be expected, nor is it intended that these hours should be adhered to in all cases and at all times, but only when regularity of hours does not interfere with the performance of police duties.

58. During the summer months no fire will be allowed in any of the apartments except the cook-house or kitchen.

59. Where it is possible, it is expected that the police will supply themselves with wood and water, but where this is not practicable, the officer in charge will make the most advantageous arrangement in his power, having due regard to economy in the expenditure of the public money.

60. The officer in charge will be held strictly responsible that the relatives of policemen, but more particularly discharged constables, or other persons not connected with the establishment, shall not be allowed to sleep in the barracks ; and that no person, except on business relating to the public service, shall be allowed to frequent police premises.

61. A man who has been dismissed from the Force must never be allowed to enter police quarters, on any excuse whatsoever; nor is any member of the Force to associate with such person, if the offence for which he was dismissed was of such a nature as to attach disgrace to the Force.

62. Every article in a barrack-room is to have its appointed place, and when not in use is not to be out of that place. Provisions are not to be exposed to view, nor are mess utensils to be left unarranged or uncleansed.

63. The officer in charge of a station is to take into his possession the private effects of any policeman who dies at such station ; and he is to make a careful inventory of such effects in the presence of a subscribing witness, and shall give a true copy of such inventory to the Inspector of his district, who is to transmit the same, with all necessary information on the subject, to the Commissioner, with a view to the proper disposal of such private effects.

64. When the importance of the barrack regulations are duly considered, it will be observed that a great responsibility rests with the officers in charge, for they will be held strictly responsible that the whole of the foregoing regulations are enforced, and that they immediately report any infraction of them.

HORSES.

65. Except where an allowance is made for horses, they will be purchased for the Force under the direction of the Commissioner, who will appoint some person to make the purchase, and the horses so procured must, in all cases where practicable, be examined by a veterinary surgeon

in conjunction with such officer of the Force as may be appointed to execute that duty, and certified to by them as being suitable for the Force, as to soundness, age, and general fitness for service, before payment is made.

66. In the event of authority being given for the purchase of horses in remote districts, the certificate must be signed by two officers, of whom the Inspector of the District must be one.

67. No pecuniary or other advantage whatever, from such purchase, is to accrue to any member of the Police Force.

68. Should it be found that any member of the Force, whether officer or otherwise, either ill-treats or permits to be ill-treated or neglected, the horse told off to him, or any other horse under his charge, he will, in addition to such other punishment as may be inflicted upon him, be dismounted, and ordered to return to foot police duty, provided he is retained in the Force.

69. No member of the foot police is to be mounted, nor is any mounted constable to be dismounted without authority from the Commissioner.

70. Each Inspector of a district will keep a register of the horses under his charge, in which their age, height, distinctive marks, branded letters and numbers are to be carefully entered, and on no occasion are the horses belonging to one district to be ridden or otherwise used by the officers or men of another.

71. A similar register must be kept by the officers in charge of stations, of the horses in their charge, for which they will be responsible to the Inspector of the district, who, in like manner, will be held accountable by the Commissioner.

72. It is expected that the Inspectors of districts will see that every horse under them, as well as its rider, shall have a fair share of the work to be done, and that they will not allow some horses to be petted and kept idle in the stables, while others are being injured by severe usage or neglect ; nor are any of the horses to be kept clothed in the stables, unless sick.

73. No horse is to travel at a pace exceeding five miles per hour, unless in cases of emergency, such as the pursuit of offenders, &c., where it is apparent that speed is absolutely necessary.

74. When any horse, from disease or injuries received, becomes totally useless, a report of the circumstance should be forwarded to the Commissioner, when an order will be given for its disposal; but in the event of a limb being fractured or any other such injury, the officer in charge will at once put an end to its misery by killing it on the spot, forwarding a report of the case in the usual manner.

75. A table stating the prescribed daily ration for each horse will be issued, and a copy thereof is to be hung up in every stable wherein a police horse is to be permanently foraged, and the constable having the charge of a horse will be held responsible that the animal receives the authorised ration.

76. No mounted constable will, on any consideration, use in harness the horse set apart for him, unless ordered to do so for Government purposes by his superior officer, nor is any member of the Force to use his horse unless in the execution of his duty.

77. Any officer or constable using a private instead of a Government horse in the discharge of his duty, must forward to the Commissioner, in the usual manner, a certificate, signed by the Inspector of the District, that the animal in question is of the proper height and appearance, and in every respect suited for the service; but he will not be allowed to make use of any Government horse in addition to his own private horse, unless in a case of emergency, when it must be shown that his own was injured in the service, or otherwise unequal to the duty required of it; nor will he be allowed to make use of the horse, so kept at the Government expense, in harness or for his private purposes, nor to dispose of it without the sanction of the Commissioner.

78. The officers are not to ride the horses told off to the men under their command, nor are police horses to be

ridden by any other member of the community, unless under special authority.

79. When a report is made by a constable or other member of the Force of the bad state or condition of his horse, the Inspector of the District will direct an immediate inquiry to be made as to the amount of duty lately performed by it, and how it has been treated by its rider.

80. In the event of any horse being sold from the Force, it will be disposed of by public auction, in such manner as the Commissioner may direct.

81. A greater number of horses will be allowed in each district than are in actual use, so that those requiring it may occasionally have rest; but should the number of mounted men in a district be reduced, the officer in charge will cause the supernumerary horses to be turned out into the nearest police paddock until he has received instructions as to their disposal; and should he be instructed to send them to the depôt, he will send with them, addressed to the officer in charge, a return, giving the names of the horses, their brands, color, age, &c. Should additional horses be required in a district, an application to that effect must be forwarded to the Commissioner.

FORAGE.

82. Members of the Force, in charge of stations, are expected to give due notice to local contractors, if any, stating the supplies of forage needed, in accordance with the terms of contract.

83. When forage is delivered at any station by a contractor, the net weight must be ascertained, and the receipt signed for that quantity, for which the officer having charge, and who signs the receipt, will, in his issues, be held responsible.

84. If a station be under the charge of a subordinate member of the Force, he should permit no one but himself to issue forage; at large stations one constable only must be authorised to issue.

85. When a fresh supply of forage is received at a station, it must not be issued until the old stock in store is consumed.

B

86. The police at every station are to exert themselves to insure the supplies being stored in such a manner as to prevent any injury through the effects of weather or other causes ; as, should any damage or loss occur, the strictest investigation will be made, and the party who, from negligence or other fault, allowed the same to take place, will be held personally liable for it.

87. At out-stations where the stores are kept in a tent, or any insecure building, the police on the station must erect a strong fence round the same to prevent any damage by cattle, &c.

88. No forage is on any account to be issued from the police stores to any Government officer or other person whatever, without special authority ; and in every instance where forage is issued for any other service than the police, a requisition must be obtained from the party requiring the same, which order must be attached to the weekly forage return, in which also care must be taken to insert the particulars of the amount of forage drawn, the officer's name, and on what duty engaged.

GENERAL RULES.

89. Every member of the Force will be required to devote his whole time and energies to the service, and will be held responsible for obedience to all lawful orders, and regulations.

90. Members of the Force, on their arrival in Brisbane, whether on duty or leave of absence, are to report themselves at the Commissioner's office. If on leave of absence, it is only necessary that they report themselves on their arrival, leaving their address, and again on their departure.

91. In the absence of any member of the Force from a district, station, or post, the duties and responsibilities will specially devolve upon the senior officer or constable next in rank.

92. Every member of the Force in charge of a station will be specially responsible for the conduct, appearance, and discipline of the constables under him, and for the state of the arms, ammunition, and other public property committed to his charge.

93. The officer in charge of police, as well as every individual policeman appointed to any district, division, or subdivision, under whatever designation, will be held responsible for the peace, good order, and security of such portion thereof as may be committed to his charge, as well as for the general performance of other police duties.

94. The officer or member of the Force in charge of police in any district will, as far as lies in his power, act in accordance with the wishes of the Bench, for which purpose he will communicate personally with the Magistrates, to ascertain if their lawful orders are duly carried out by the members of the Force; whether they are active, diligent, and efficient in the prevention of crime or the pursuit of criminals, and orderly, respectful, and steady in their conduct.

95. Every member of the Force must pay strict and prompt obedience to all the lawful orders and directions of the Police Magistrate or Bench of Magistrates.

96. Cases of breach of police discipline or regulations, insubordination, or disputes between members of the Force, will be dealt with by the Police Magistrate, or, in his absence, by any other officer of police; offences against the public, or when Magistrates have clear jurisdiction as under 27 Victoria, No. 11, clause XIII, and elsewhere, will be always submitted to two local Magistrates, or the Bench of Magistrates, unconnected with the Force.

97. All members of the Force in charge of a district will attend at the police court, for the purpose of assisting in carrying out the views of the Magistrates, and will also report personally to the Magistrates, on their assembling, the results of all warrants and processes issued, and the steps taken to give effect to their judicial proceedings.

98. All communications which the officers in charge of the districts may wish to be made known to the Government, or to the head of any other department, should be forwarded through the Commissioner of Police.

99. Every member of the Force will be presumed to know his duty in every case, and in the absence of orders or instructions will be held responsible for the due performance thereof, and in case of failure or neglect will be liable to punishment and dismissal.

100. In every case of neglect or failure of duty by a subordinate the officer responsible will make a record thereof, and report the same with as little delay as possible, to the Commissioner.

101. Every officer or member of the Force will keep a correct register of all furniture or other Government property under his charge, and in the event of being transferred to another station will obtain a receipt for the same from his successor.

102. The engagement of any member of the Police Force will be for óne year, and thereafter, until legally discharged.

103. Any member who shall be dismissed cannot be again admitted into the Police Force.

GENERAL DUTIES OF THE DIFFERENT RANKS.

COMMISSIONER.

104. The Commissioner is appointed, under the authority of the Act of Parliament 27 Victoria, No 11, to have the superintendence, under the direction of the Colonial Secretary, of the Police Force of the whole Colony, including the Native Police Force. He will be held specially responsible for the peace and good order of the Colony, and in general for the discipline and organization of the Force. He will take every step in his power to cause all under his control to discharge their duties, both to the public and the Government, satisfactorily and efficiently.

105. He will furnish the Government with a quarterly report of the general state of the Police Force (including

the Native Police), as to the number of men and horses, their distribution and general efficiency, the increase or diminution of crime, the number of new stations that may have been formed, with such other information as it may be necessary to afford. An annual report shall also be laid before Parliament.

DUTIES OF POLICE MAGISTRATES APPOINTED TO ACT AS INSPECTORS OF POLICE.

106. A Police Magistrate when gazetted to the office of Inspector of Police shall be responsible for the prevention of crime, the detection of criminals, the general preservation of peace and order within his district, and for the general conduct and efficiency of the members of the Force immediately under his charge.

107. He will make himself acquainted with the manner in which the police duties are performed by all grades of the Force within his district, both towards the Magistracy and the public, and shall periodically forward, for the information of the Government, the opinion of the "Bench" in his district as to the manner in which the police duties are carried on.

108. A Police Magistrate acting as Inspector, unless specially instructed otherwise, will be exempt from the ordinary duties performed by the officers of the Force; but when emergencies arise, or riots are apprehended, he will then be required to act in immediate charge of the Police Force, both as an Inspector, as well as in his magisterial capacity.

109. He will see that the senior member of the Force within his district fulfils his duties as laid down in these Regulations, and will satisfy himself that the necessary books are kept, and the periodical returns duly made.

INSPECTOR.

110. The Inspector is to reside constantly within in his district, and not to leave it except by permission from the Colonial Secretary; and whenever he leaves the head quarters for other parts of the district, he will report the same, and also his return.

111. The duties of the Inspector are those of direction, of constant and active supervision and inspection, requiring his movements to be rapid and uncertain, and his vigilance unrelaxing.

112. The Inspector will make himself acquainted with the various stations in the district, and their requirements generally, and will from time to time, according to his discretion, grant immediate police protection to any locality that may require it, if it is apparent that the peace of the locality would be endangered by the delay consequent upon his referring the matter to head-quarters for instructions.

113. It is not possible exactly to define his responsibility, but he is bound to see that all under his control discharge their respective duties towards the public with zeal, fidelity, and efficiency ; and it is expected he will at all times ready and able to afford advice and information on any matter relating to their public duties.

114. As the advancement in the service of those under his command will very much depend on his recommendations, he will be particular to ascertain their relative merits and qualifications for promotion.

115. As he is responsible for the general conduct and good order of the officers and constables under his command, he should make himself well acquainted by frequent personal intercourse with the Sub-Inspectors and sergeants, and through them with the character, temper, and conduct of each constable ; he will be firm and just, and at the same time kind and conciliating towards them in his behavior, on all occasions.

116. Much must be done by himself, and under his own immediate inspection. As he is held responsible for the general performance of police duties within his own district, he must give clear and precise instructions to the officers under him, and report every instance of neglect to the Commissioner.

117. He will feel the importance of visiting the stations, watch-houses, &c., in his district at uncertain times, and as often as possible, when he will see that they are kept

clean and in proper order, and will inspect the books, and see that they are kept in a correct, neat, and regular manner; inserting his opinion of the whole in the Station Occurrence Book, and reporting every irregularity or neglect of the barrack regulations or discipline which may appear to him on such inspection.

118. He must see that the men are acquainted with the use and management of their arms and appointments, and with their general duties, and that the constabulary at the several stations are well acquainted with the roads and the bush, so as to enable them to move by the shortest line to any required point.

119. He will strictly examine the roster of duties, to see that they have been arranged with perfect impartiality; he will also inquire of the men whether they have any complaints, and will at once investigate them if preferred.

120. He will see that at the various stations a proper system of patrols is established, so that as far as possible the whole of the district may be properly guarded.

121. He will strictly satisfy himself that officers and constables have not, by contracting debts to publicans and others, or by incurring obligations of any kind, placed themselves in a position calculated in any degree to shackle their exertions, or to impair their efficiency in discharging the duties of their office.

122. He is to pay strict and constant attention to economy, and whenever he sees any means of reducing the expense and promoting the utility of the Force in the locality within his charge, he should not fail to communicate his views to the Commissioner.

123. He will be held responsible for a careful scrutiny of all estimates, accounts, and vouchers connected with the Force under him, which are to be supported and authenticated by his certificate of approval; and that all accounts, returns, reports, and other official documents, are drawn up and perfected with the greatest accuracy, precision, and neatness, and transmitted punctually at the proper periods.

124. On the transference, retirement, or removal from the service of any officer under him, he will cause all

public records, books, or other documents, the property of the public, in that officer's possession, to be handed by him to his successor; and on the Inspector himself giving up the charge of a district from any of the above causes, he will in like manner hand all public records, books, and documents to the officer relieving him.

125. On the receipt of an order for the discharge or dismissal of any member of the Force, he will order the party in to head-quarters, when he will see that all his arms, accoutrements, &c., are given into store complete and in good condition. He will then pay such salary as may still be due, unless the same has been forfeited.

·126. On the transference of any sergeant or constable from one district to another, he will send, under cover, to the officer in charge of the district to which the party is transferred, his defaulter's sheet, together with his register, in proper form, detailing his name, description, date up to which paid, &c., &c.

127. Should it be necessary for the Inspector to leave the district, the Sub-Inspector of the district will take charge until the return of the Inspector, or the appointment of some other officer to it. Also, when the Inspector is absent from head-quarters, inspecting the stations in the district, or on other duty, the same officer will assume charge, so that as a rule the Inspector or Sub-Inspector will always be in charge at head-quarters.

128. The Inspector will make a report, in writing, as early as possible, of any complaint of misconduct on the part of any member of the Force, which it has been considered necessary to refer to a Bench of Magistrates for adjudication; and will also, if necessary, suspend from duty the individual against whom a complaint has been made, waiting the decision of the Commissioner; but in no case will he dismiss or discharge any member of the Force without due authority.

129. Any member of the Force suspended from duty, although not performing any police duty, will remain within the limits of the station to which he belongs, unless under orders to the contrary, and will not be entitled to

salary for the time he remains suspended, unless by special authority from the Commissioner.

130. It is of great importance that Government should receive immediate intelligence of every occurrence involving the safety of person or property, or the maintenance of the public peace, and, whenever practicable, such intelligence is to be communicated by the electric telegraph to the Commissioner.

131. The Inspector will see that the members of the Force under his command exert themselves to the utmost, not only in the prevention of crime, which is their principal duty, but also in its detection, and will be answerable for their general conduct and good order.

132. He will cause the men, when they have cases to bring before the bench, to be instructed how to obtain evidence, so as to present the particulars to the magistrates as clearly and intelligibly as possible. He will not only give directions to this effect to the constables, but will also see the necessity of attending the police court himself as frequently as possible, to see that his instructions are carried into effect.

133. Each Inspector will see that the following books are properly kept by the Sub-Inspector :—

> General order book, to contain copies of all general orders that may from time to time be received from the Commissioner's office.
> District order book, to contain copies of all other orders.
> Letter and minute book.
> Warrant book.
> Registry of horses.
> Miscellaneous property book.
> Store book.

134. He will also make the following periodical returns :—

> Weekly return of duty performed by men and horses, and persons apprehended at each station.
> Monthly general report to be furnished on the 1st of each month, accompanied by the following returns :—

(1.) Return of warrants received, executed, and remaining unexecuted ; specifying the names, offences, and results.

(2.) Pay and allowance abstracts, in duplicate.

A return of arms, ammunition, and handcuffs, &c., is to be forwarded to the Commissioner every six months.

135. The duty returns will be kept by the officers or sergeants in charge of the stations, and, as well as the above-mentioned books, must be examined and certified by the Inspector.

136. Copies or duplicates of all returns made by the Inspectors are to be kept by them.

137. No officer will be allowed the services of a member of the Force as clerk, without express permission from the Commissioner.

138. In order to maintain, as nearly as practicable, one uniform and complete system throughout the establishment, the Inspectors are to refrain from making any regulations or issuing any orders which may be calculated to produce alterations or cause innovations in the standing orders of the Force.

139. Whenever, in the opinion of the Inspector, it may be expedient to introduce any new regulation, or to alter an old one, he should submit his ideas on the subject for the consideration of the Commissioner, who, should he deem the proposition advisable, will carry it into effect by a general order ; this, however, is not to be understood as extending to an order of a temporary nature ; but a copy of any such temporary order is to be sent to the Commissioner's office.

SUB-INSPECTOR.

140. The Sub-Inspector will be held responsible for the conduct and appearance of the constables, and for the state of the barracks and quarters, the arms, ammunition, appointments, &c., at the principal stations in the district ; and where there is a police paddock, he must take care that the fencing is kept in good order, making the constables execute any necessary repairs at times when not on other duty.

141. He is to a great extent responsible for the drill of the men of the district, and is selected expressly on account of superior knowledge of his duties.

142. He must keep a roster of duties performed by himself and the men under him, and will see that those constables who have to give evidence at the police court are in attendance and properly dressed.

143. He will attend daily at the Inspector's office with reports of such constables under him as may have misconducted themselves, and will cause to be in attendance those parties who can give evidence.

144. He will inspect all horses, &c., belonging to the Force which may arrive at and leave the station, and will see that the horses are properly groomed and attended to, and that everything is kept in proper order.

145. He will frequently, and at uncertain hours, inspect the quarters of the sergeants and men, and will occasionally visit them during meals, for the purpose of seeing on such occasions that the men are properly and cleanly dressed, and conduct themselves in a proper manner.

146. His position is looked upon, to a certain extent, as a confidential one;. and he will therefore do all in his power to preserve regularity and order, and to make himself acquainted with anything to the contrary which he thinks should be brought to the notice of the Inspector or other officer under whom he may be placed.

147. In the absence of the Inspector, the Sub-Inspector is to represent that officer, and therefore what has been stated of the duties of the Inspector, as to discipline, applies equally to the Sub-Inspector when in the temporary charge of a district or station.

148. It is his peculiar province to watch over the conduct of the constables, and to report every irregularity, neglect of duty, or breach of discipline they commit, to the Inspector, without delay.

149. His conduct towards the Inspector must be respectful and obedient, whilst to the men he is to be civil and obliging, without compromising the respect due to his rank by improper familiarity.

150. He is never to absent himself from his station, except on duty, or by permission or direction of the Inspector of his district, and he must at all times be ready to meet any demand upon his services.

151. He must be perfectly impartial in the division of all the duties of his station.

152. He will be held strictly responsible for the appearance of his men and barracks, the state of the arms, ammunition, appointments, and every article of Government property, committed to his charge. He must show an example of neatness in his dress and appointments, and of perfect cleanliness in his person and quarters ; and if he suffers any disobedience of orders or neglect of duty, without immediately reporting to his Inspector, he will be considered unfit for the position of Sub-Inspector, and be reduced accordingly.

153. He is occasionally to wait on the police or local magistrates, to receive their instructions ; and it is of the utmost importance that he should take every pains to inform himself of the several roads, passes, residences, and characters of his neighborhood.

154. He is to report to the local bench, as well as to his Inspector, all outrages or other matters connected with the tranquillity of his district, and shall visit the scenes of all outrages as soon as possible, without reference to districts and stations, unless he shall have reason to know that the place had been visited by some other responsible party.

155. He will pay particular attention to the public houses and other places of entertainment within the limits of his charge, and will report any irregularity he may observe to the Inspector under whom he is placed.

156. He will keep the books, and make periodical returns to the Inspector, as enumerated in the instructions to that officer.

157. It will be his duty to make himself acquainted with the characters of the several public-houses, or other licensed places of entertainment and amusement in his district, in order that he may be in a position to afford the

necessary information to the magistrates on the days appointed for granting or renewing licenses, and will report any irregularity to the Inspector.

158. When prisoners are remanded from one bench of magistrates to another, the Sub-Inspector, or officer in charge of the station, will forward to the officer in charge of police at the place to which the prisoner is remanded, the full particulars of the case, stating why the prisoner has been remanded, with any other information he may be able to afford.

159. Money or other property which may come into the possession of the police, and respecting the disposal of which there may be some doubt, is to be forwarded, together with a report of the circumstances, to headquarters, with a view to its being disposed of as may be directed by some competent authority.

160. He is to forward all notices of resignation, and all correspondence, accounts, vouchers, and returns intended for the Commissioner's office, to the Inspector, in proper form, and at the regulated periods.

161. In case of criminal offences, however, a copy of the information to be communicated should be sent direct to the Commissioner's office, as the delay which would otherwise occur might be prejudical to the public service.

SERGEANTS.

162. The sergeant is the immediate assistant of the Sub-Inspector, if at the same station; if detached, his duties are, in fact, those of an acting Sub-Inspector, and he must be governed by the general spirit and principles of the instructions for that officer.

163. He must be perfectly impartial in the division of all the duties of his station, taking his own regular turn of them.

164. He must in his own person set an example of activity, zeal, strict attention to duty, and unvarying propriety of conduct.

165. He must keep a diary of the duties performed by himself and the men at his station.

166. He will be held strictly responsible to the Sub-Inspector for the conduct and appearance of his constables, for the state of the barracks or quarters, the arms, amunition, appointments, &c.

167. He is to inspect minutely all parties or individuals going on duty, and if under arms, is to count the amunition in their pouches before they go out and when they return, noting in the occurrence book the hour of their despatch and return, the state of the men and horses, if they or any of them be mounted, and all circumstances connected with the peculiar duty on which they had been employed of which a record may appear in any degree necessary.

168. When the number of sergeants in a district is insufficient to place one in charge of each station, the Inspector, or officer in charge of the district, will select the best conducted and most efficient constables to take charge; and on such constables will devolve all the duties of a sergeant, and they will receive a trifling addition to their pay, and as vacancies occur, will be promoted to the rank of sergeant.

CONSTABLES.

169. The constable, though frequently acting on specific orders applicable to the occasion, is very generally, in the execution of his duty as a peace officer, called upon to act on his own responsibility; he therefore requires discretion, intelligence, decision, and perfect command of temper. His first duty is perfect obedience to his superiors; he should receive the orders of those above him with deference and respect, and execute them to the very best of his power. He is to be ever on the alert for the prevention of crime and the protection of person and property, and is never to omit to report to his sergeant, Sub-Inspector, or Inspector, any circumstances which may, in the most remote degree, appear to affect the public peace or the character of the Force.

170. All constables will, on arrival at a station, immediately report themselves to the senior officer in charge;

and, should they remain longer than twenty-four hours, will take their turn of duty with the men on the station.

171. It is of great importance that the constables should be respected by all classes, and obtain their good opinion. They will therefore be extremely cautious in their demeanor, and by sober, orderly, and regular habits, and ready zeal to execute the lawful orders and commands of the magistrates, endeavor to obtain their approbation.

172. As no man can be promoted to the rank of sergeant, no matter how exemplary his conduct, who cannot write a good official report or letter, it is the interest of every constable to devote such hours as he can spare from his duty to reading and writing.

173. The constable must not incur debts to publicans, storekeepers, or others in the district, nor place himself in any way under obligations which would necessary shackle and impair his efficiency and impartiality.

174. If employed as a mounted constable, he must on all occasions be most careful and attentive to his horse, saddle, and accoutrements; any mounted man neglecting, or abusing, or who is deficient in kindness to his horse, will be at once dismounted, and subject to punishment. For any loss or injury to his horse, saddlery, arms, or appointments, by any neglect on his part, the constable will be held responsible. *

175. It is indispensably necessary that he should make himself perfectly acquainted with all the parts of his beat or section, with the streets, thoroughfares, courts, and houses.

176. He will be expected to possess such a knowledge of the inhabitants of each house as to enable him to recognize their persons, and thus prevent mistakes, and be enabled to render assistance to the inhabitants when called for.

177. He should see every part of his beat -in the time allotted, and this he will be expected to do regularly, so that any person requiring assistance, by remaining in the same spot for that length of time, may meet a constable. This regularity of moving through his beat shall not, however, prevent his remaining at any particular place, if his presence there be necessary for the due performance of his

duty, to observe the conduct of any suspected person, or for any other good reason; but he will be required to satisfy his sergeant or superior officer that there was a sufficient couse for such apparent irregularity.

178. He will also attend at the appointed times to make a report to his sergeant of anything requiring notice.

179. If at any time he requires immediate assistance, and cannot in any other way obtain it, he must sound his whistle, but this is to be done as seldom as possible; for though he is provided with one, and may sometimes find it necessary to use it, such alarm frequently creates the inconvenience it is intended to prevent, by assembling a crowd. He will require to report to the sergeant every occasion of using his whistle.

180. He should clearly understand what powers are given him by law for the efficient execution of his duties, and for this purpose, extracts from the different Acts of Parliament conferring powers on the police, under their proper headings, with instructions for their guidance, will be supplied to every member of the Force.

181. Every person taken into custody without warrant (except persons detained for the mere purpose of ascertaining their name or residence), is to be forthwith taken to the watchhouse.

182. When a constable takes any one into custody, he should, if possible, before he leaves his beat, give notice to another constable, who can supply his place while he is taking the party to the watchhouse, and he will return again to his duty as soon as possible; or he may, when not himself required as a witness on the charge, deliver over his prisoner to the sergeant or other constable, and immediately return to his beat; but it is generally most advisable that he should accompany the party to the watchhouse, in order to substantiate the charge.

183. No constable is to search a prisoner by himself, but in all cases must take him to the nearest watchhouse or police quarters, and in the presence of the watchhouse-keeper or a sergeant, will take from him all property in his possession. Before confining the prisoner in the watchhouse the property must be given to the watchhouse-

keeper, and entered by him in the " charge book," which
must be signed by the prisoner, if he is willing, but if not,
by the sergeant or watchhouse-keeper and the apprehend-
ing constable. The watchhouse-keeper will be held
responsible that all prisoners are thoroughly searched.

184. A constable is not to leave his beat during his
tour of duty, unless under the circumstances already
mentioned, or others which may make it necessary. He
shall not enter any house except in the execution of his
duty.

185. He will pay particular attention to all public-
houses within his beat, reporting the hour at which each
is closed, and whether they appear to be conducted in an
orderly manner.

186. On no pretence shall a constable enter any public-
house, except in the immediate execution of his duty.
Such a breach of positive order will not be excused, and
he subjects the publican himself to a severe fine for
allowing him to remain there.

187. If he observes anything in the street likely to
produce danger or public inconvenience, or anything
which seems to him irregular and offensive, he must report
it to the sergeant.

188. He must not, when on duty, enter into conversation with any person whatever, except on matters relative
to his duty ; and when asked by any person his name and
number, &c., he will immediately give them.

189. He must be particularly cautious not to interfere
unnecessarily ; but when required to act, is to do so with
decision and boldness, but without unnecessary violence.
He will be civil and attentive to all persons of every rank
and class ; insolence and incivility will not be passed over.
In the proper exercise of his authority, on all occasions,
he may expect to receive full support.

ESCORTS.

190. Escorts form a very important part of the duty of
the police.

191. The first consideration, and that which must never
be lost sight of by escorts, is the security of the prisoners

or commodities placed in their charge; to this all else must be secondary and subordinate. The first point, therefore, to be looked to by the constabulary when employed on this duty is, that the prisoners or property they are to escort are delivered to them with due precautions for safe custody, and this they are to state in the receipt they give on taking them over.

192. Whoever delivers to any escort prisoners or property, must at the same time prescribe the nature and degree of personal restraint to be imposed on prisoners, and the description of boxes and packages containing, and the fastenings securing property, and neither should be deviated from, or in any way altered by the escort or successive escorts in whose charge they are placed, unless under such circumstances of necessity as will fully justify the act. In all such cases the escort, or person in charge of the escort, making the alteration, will report clearly and at length upon the matter.

193. Having thus received their charge properly secured, it will be their duty, and consequently their responsibility, to guard against that state of security being diminished or impaired ; for this purpose, they will frequently and closely inspect the handcuffs, chains, &c., placed on the prisoners, and the fastenings of doors, windows, &c., of any place of confinement. In like manner as regards property, they will inspect the locks, seals, or other means by which the boxes or packages are secured. Neither by day or by night must their charge be separate from, or lost sight of by an escort.

194. There may be occasions for escorts to stop during the night at public-houses ; this, however. must never be done when it can be possibly avoided, but when such a step is absolutely necessary, an agreement must be made with the proprietor of the house for the use of a room, and for meals supplied to prisoners, on the most moderate terms.

195. In such cases they are not to drink, nor allow the prisoners in their charge to drink, any fermented or spirituous liquors whatever; they are to place the prisoners in the most secure and private rooms obtainable,

and are to adopt all proper and necessary precautions against escape.

196. Escorts, with prisoners or property in charge, are not to call or halt at public-houses during the day. The necessary provisions and refreshments must be procured at, and taken with them from, the place which they have stopped at on the previous night.

197. On the march, they will keep the prisoners in the centre of the party, and will not allow them to separate or straggle, and therefore the rate of marching must be regulated according to the powers of the prisoners, if on foot, and if in carts, according to the pace at which the vehicles can conveniently proceed. Neither acquaintances of the prisoners, nor other persons, are to be allowed to mix with, or accompany the prisoners and escort.

198. The arms of an escort are invariably to be loaded; they must be kept from wet as much as possible, and always in a state for instant use. After rain they must be examined, and if the powder in the nipples appears in the least damp, the charge must be drawn, and the arms thoroughly cleaned, dried, and re-loaded. This, of course, applies more particularly to cases where treasure, or prisoners in custody on a charge of felony are being escorted; but in escorting females, lunatics, or persons charged with some trifling misdemeanor, it will not for the most part be necessary that the escort be provided with firearms.

199. It must, however, be clearly understood and constantly borne in mind, that nothing short of absolute and inevitable necessity can justify the police in firing upon prisoners endeavoring to escape, or upon other parties attempting to rescue.

200. As prisoners are not on any account to be left in the possession of money or other property when under escort, everything belonging to them is to be made up into separate sealed packages, marked with the name of the prisoner and the amount, and these separate parcels (with a list) enclosed in a strong sealed cover; a memorandum is to be delivered with this sealed parcel to the officer in charge, his acknowledgment and signature being

taken to a duplicate retained. This memorandum and the sealed parcel he is to hand, with the seal unbroken, to the person into whose charge he delivers the prisoners, taking his receipt for it.

201. The officer in charge of a party on escort duty should always march in the rear of such escort, and enforce a strict attention to the duty on the part of the men, who should not be allowed to straggle under any pretence.

202. Before taking charge of prisoners, for the purpose of conveying them from one place to another, the officer in charge of the escort will be particular that they are searched in his presence, and that he receives the proper authority for their custody, whether they may be remanded from one bench to another or under sentence. In every case, the officer in charge will examine the warrants or other authority, to see that they correspond with the prisoners handed over to their charge.

203. When taking charge of gold, specie, or other treasure, or Government parcels, he must be particular that the same are duly entered in the way-bill, and to obtain a receipt for them from the party to whom he delivers the articles.

204. Where practicable, after having given up charge of property or prisoners entrusted to them, the parties composing the escort will return to their stations by twos, starting at different hours, and where convenient by different roads, the officer in charge of the escort forming one of the last party, so that he may be able to check any irregularity that may take place. In this manner they will form an efficient patrol.

205. Any constable accompanying a Judge when on circuit, or any Government officer, as an orderly, should be relieved at each station, so as to avoid as much as possible taking any man to a distance from his station or into another district.

206. No officer of the Force or police magistrate is, under any circumstances, to be accompanied by a constable as orderly. When an officer has to perform any duty in which his personal safety is endangered, he may

take with him one or more constables, as the necessity of
the case may require ; but under such circumstances the
constable or constables will precede instead of following
him, as the attendance of constables on officers as a mark
of honor is strictly forbidden.

PATROLS.

207. The duties of a district cannot be performed
efficiently without the establishment of a proper system
of patrolling, which should be carried out under the
general instructions of the Inspector, so that the patrols
from the different stations may be regulated with a view
to general co-operation.

208. The particulars of every patrol made from a station
will be entered in the " occurrence book " of the station—
the hours at which patrols have been made from each
station, the places visited, and the incidents which have
occurred to the patrols—so that the officers in charge
may be enabled to form a return of the patrolling which
has taken place at stations. He can then regulate it with
a due regard to the requirements of the service and the
extent of duty which the men are called on to perform.

209. This duty, to be performed efficiently, must be
performed silently, and without any sign of preparation
which can attract attention, and put ill-disposed persons
upon their guard.

210. Patrols are not to go out on stated nights, or at
particular hours, but at irregular periods, and are always
to visit suspected places, and observe suspicious houses
and persons.

211. They will not confine their attention to the main
lines of road only, but will occasionally proceed through
the bush, calling at the houses of the settlers to find out
what is going on, to ascertain if their assistance is required,
or to obtain any information they can relative to horse
and cattle stealers, or any other offenders.

212. If disorderly and suspicious persons are met by
patrols at unseasonable hours, they are to be apprehended
and brought before a magistrate for examination.

213. In certain cases it may be more conducive to the objects of patrols to conceal themselves near suspected passes or places than to prolong their march along a public road ; when so concealed the strictest silence must be observed.

214. When on patrol duty, constables are not to smoke, to separate, nor talk loudly, or enter public-houses except in the performance of their duty.

DUTIES AT THE WATCHHOUSE.

215. A constable must always be on duty at the station-house, who is on no account to quit it during his time of duty.

216. He will receive all charges against prisoners brought in by the different constables or other individuals, ascertain their nature, and when he is satisfied that it is a proper charge, cause the name of each prisoner to be entered, with the particulars of his offence, in a book which he shall keep for the purpose, to be called the "charge book."

217. He shall not receive into custody any person brought in by a police constable on the vague charge of *obstructing* the constable in the execution of his duty, unless it be accompanied by a specification of particulars.

218. He may admit to bail, with the consent of the officer on duty, persons charged during the night-time with any petty misdemeanor, such as trifling assaults, committing trifling wilful mischief, and others of a similar description ; also, persons charged with drunkenness may, when they become sober, be admitted to bail, as in other cases of petty misdemeanor.

219. Persons against whom charges for assault attended by cutting and wounding have been received, or for felonies, or aggravated misdemeanors, when the charge has been received and entered in the "charge book," are to be detained in custody at the watchhouse until they can be taken before a magistrate for examination ; and no prisoner can be detained in the custody of the police after he has been once brought before a magistrate to

answer the charge preferred against him, without a warrant for his detention.

220. Persons apprehended on warrant should only be admitted to bail with the sanction of the magistrate by whom the warrant was signed, or, in his absence, by an rder from the Inspector or officer in charge of the istrict; except in cases of persons being taken into custody for indictable offences, whether by warrant or otherwise, who are not to be discharged on bail until they have been brought before the bench, and bail ordered by the magistrates.

221. When a person is accused of having committed a felony or misdemeanor (as the case may be), and there is reasonable ground for preferring the complaint, inquiry as to the fact is to be made only of the person who prefers the complaint (who does so on his own responsibility), and is not to be made of other persons, although they may be cognisant of them; but in a subsequent stage of the proceedings, before the magistrate, they may be heard as witnesses. For this purpose their names and addresses, if they are in attendance at the watchhouse, should be entered in the " charge book."

222. If a complainant, after having given a person into custody, on a criminal charge, should refuse to sign it in the " charge] book," supposing the charge to have been made in the first instance to a constable, the constable shall, if he has seen the offence committed, enter and sign the charge himself, and the complainant may be summoned before the magistrate to substantiate it. The sergeant on duty, or watchhouse keeper, is, for this purpose, always to ascertain the name and address of the party complaining, previously to his making any inquiry of him. If the constable is himself unable to establish the charge, and the complainant refuses to support it, the party accused is not to be detained, save when the offence is serious, and there are grounds to suppose the prisoner guilty, notwithstanding the prosecutor's refusal to sign the charge.

223. If the complaint in the first instance is not made by a third person, but by a constable on his own view, the

charge is to be received, entered in the " charge book,"
and submitted to the magistrate; but if it should turn out,
upon the statement of the constable, that in point of fact
there are not reasonable grounds for suspecting that the
offence has been committed by the person arrested, he
must be discharged, and a full report of the particulars
of the case made in writing to the Inspector. This power
of inquiry and discharge by the officer on duty is necessary to protect the public against the ignorance or
improper behaviour of constables.

224. If any property be brought to the constable on duty
at the watchhouse, either taken from persons apprehended
or otherwise, he will immediately make an entry of the
same in the "charge book," and the several articles of
property are to be marked at the time they are received,
so that they may be afterwards certainly known to be the
same. They should be taken by the watchhouse-keeper
himself from the person bringing them, and not allowed
to be out of his sight until marked in the manner directed ;
they should then be locked up in the place for the purpose,
or in certain cases, when required as evidence, given back
to the charge of the constable who took possession of
them.

225. When any person who may be brought to the
watchhouse in a state of intoxication is searched, which
should be at the watchhouse (except in particular cases
where immediate search becomes necessary), the articles
should always be taken by one person, and called out
distinctly and entered in the book by another; and when
the person from whom they are taken is discharged, he
should sign a book or receipt for the whole. No part of
such property is to be returned to the prisoner until the
decision of the magistrate on the case is known. The
watchhouse-keeper will be held responsible that all
prisoners are thoroughly searched before being locked up.

226. As a confession from a prisoner in custody on a
charge of felony, to be admissable as evidence against
himself, must be free and voluntary, that is, must not be
extracted by any sort of threat or violence, nor obtained
by any direct or implied promises, it is advisable that in

such cases, the constable shall fix in his memory any conversation immediately preceding, so as to be able to prove it in connection with the detailed confession.

227. The authorised daily allowance of rations to prisoners confined in watchhouses is as follows :—

No. 1.—The rations to prisoners detained as witnesses, or for want of bail, when authorised to receive it :—

20 ozs. bread, 3rd quality, or 1lb. of flour	½ oz. salt
8 ozs. maize meal, or 6 ozs. of flour	1 oz. sugar
16 ozs. fresh meat	¼ oz. soup.

This ration is only issued at watchhouses on the order of a magistrate.

No. 2.—The ration to prisoners confined in solitary cells or watchhouses :—

24 ozs. bread, 3rd quality ; or 20 ozs. flour, 3rd quality.

228. The officers in charge of police at the stations where there are lock-ups, and where no Government contract exists, will call for tenders for these supplies, according to the above scale, and will transmit such tenders as they may receive to the Commissioner's office, in the usual manner. As soon as the acceptance of any tender has been notified, the rations may be ordered by the officer in charge of the station, and the account rendered to the Inspector of the district, and by him forwarded to the Commissioner's office for payment.

229. No person in the employment of Government shall have any interest in such contracts.

230. No other provisions or refreshments can be admitted into the cells, unless on the order of a medical man.

231. Prisoners in the watchhouse must be frequently visited, and immediate attention given to any case requiring assistance or medical aid.

WITNESSES AND PROSECUTORS.

232. In all trials wherein the police may be either witnesses or prosecutors, they should give their testimony in a manly, straightforward manner, without caring, or appearing to care, about the effects of it, either as to the conviction or acquittal of the accused in criminal matters, or as to its result in any civil or other suit.

233. They should merely and briefly answer the questions put to them, without remark or commentary, and if cross-examined, they should carefully avoid making a disrespectful or intemperate reply ; for if their testimony be fairly and honestly given, they need not fear, and should not be annoyed at any ordeal to which they may be subjected?

234. It must, however, be clearly understood that no man can be considered as a worthy member of the Force who is not a respectable witness, and that any instance of prevarication before any court of assize, sessions, inquiry, or tribunal whatsoever, will insure the immediate punishment of the witness who prevaricates or gives partial or vindictive evidence.

235. Any member of the police who shall have arrested an individual or individuals committed or bound for trial at assizes or circuit courts, must be considered a witness in the case whether summoned or not.

236. When members of the Force are subpœnaed as witnesses in civil cases, the amount of their expenses should be paid by the party who has subpœnaed them.

CONVEYANCE OF LETTERS AND DESPATCHES.

237. When it is absolutely necessary to send a letter or other document from one part of the country to another by despatch, it should be sent by a mounted constable to the next police station, to be given over to the officer in charge there, when the constable will return to the station from which he started, and the officer to whom the letter was delivered will, in like manner, forward it to the next station, and thus it will be forwarded to its destination without any constable being taking further than from his own station to the next.

238. When despatches are thus forwarded from station to station, written instructions, called a "route," will accompany the despatch, and in it should be stated the time of starting, the rate per mile at which it is to be carried, and whether it is to be conveyed during the night. The time of the receipt of the letter, and of its despatch from each station, will be entered in the "route" by the officer

in charge of the station, who will also make such remarks as he may consider advisable as to the condition in which the man and horse arrived. This " route" should be carefully preserved, in case of its being necessary to referto it.

239. No officer is to forward a despatch by means of a mounted mán, unless it is of so urgent a nature as to require a more speedy delivery than could otherwise be obtained ; and every such letter shall be endorsed "Urgent," and have the name of the writer written on its cover ; and every officer so forwarding a despatch will be held responsible that there was a sufficient cause of urgency to justify his having done so. If the line of stations is not specified, the officer in charge of each station where the despatch arrives will use his discretion in forwarding it to the next, by the best line for its reaching its destination.

240. The weekly reports, returns, &c., when not sent by post, can for the most part be forwarded to headquarters by the usual patrols, without the necessity of despatching a special messenger.

INSTRUCTIONS RESPECTING CORRESPONDENCE, REPORTS, ETC.

241. All letters and reports from any district, for transmission to the Commissioner's office, should be forwarded through the Inspector of the district, except in case of outrage, serious breach of the public peace, or in any matter of an urgent nature, when officers in charge of stations are to report direct to the Commissioner.

242. All correspondence and reports must be expressed in clear and concise terms, and should be written in a neat and legible hand on foolscap paper, with one-third margin.

243. Reports from subordinate members of the Force should be drawn up in the third person, according to the following form :—

" Police Station,

18 .

" Constable [or sergeant, &c., as the case may be],
" No.   reports

244. Reports relating to outrage upon person or property, or to the peace of the country, although conveyed in concise terms, should embrace a full statement of facts, and of such other particulars as may enable the Government to form a correct opinion upon the case. In every instance of crime the officer should state in his report whether any and what clue has been obtained to the discovery of the perpetrators, and the steps which have been adopted to trace out the offenders, and should also inform the police of the neighboring district or station of the particulars of the offence.

245. In referring to communications previously received from head-quarters, officers are enjoined to quote, not only the date of such communications, but also the numbers and letters which they may have borne, if any; and when any communication is forwarded with a minute, the party receiving it will, after noting and attending to it, return it without delay to the person by whom it was forwarded.

246. In forwarding the usual returns, or any returns which may be called for by the Commissioner, it is not required that they shall be accompanied by any communication, unless it may be necessary to give some explanation or information respecting such returns.

INSTRUCTIONS FOR THE GUIDANCE OF OFFICERS CHARGED WITH THE PAYMENT OF POLICE SALARIES AND CONTINGENCIES, AND THE PREPARATION OF VOUCHERS, RETURNS, AND REQUISITIONS.

PAY ABSTRACTS.

247. All abstracts of the salaries of police magistrates, clerks of petty sessions, and the constabulary generally, are to be transmitted monthly, in duplicate, to the Commissioner of Police, after careful examination by the clerk of petty sessions, and with the certificate of a magistrate thereto.

248. A reference to all new appointments not usually *gazetted* should be made on the back of the pay abstract in accordance with the instructions printed thereon, together with a memorandum notifying exchanges, resignations, or dismissals.

CONTINGENCIES.

249. Vouchers for allowances to constables when absent at night on duty, and for keeping horses, are to be forwarded with the salary abstracts, monthly, in duplicate. All other contingent vouchers should be transmitted to the Commissioner of Police quarterly, also in duplicate.

250. The allowance to a constable absent from his station on duty is two shillings per night, provided he has not been within seven (7) miles of his quarters.

251. This allowance is not made when a constable attends as a witness at the Supreme and Circuit Courts, and his expenses paid as such, or is a passenger on board a steamer or other vessel, and his passage paid by the Government.

252. The allowance for forage, &c., is at the rate of £20 per annum, and each constable receiving this allowance is bound to maintain a horse and equipments always ready for service.

253. The authorised daily allowances of fuel and light to the courthouses and watchhouses throughout the Colony are as follow, viz. :—

Courthouses.

Brisbane and Ipswich	...	...	288 lbs. wood.
Other Districts	...	...	96 do.

Watchhouses.

Summer ... ... 90 lbs. wood, ½ gill oil, daily.
(1st October to 31st May.) ·

Winter ... ... 180 lbs. wood, ⅔ gill oil, daily.
(1st June to 30th September.)

1 gill oil equivalent to 4 ozs. candles.

In places where wood can be procured without much difficulty, the police will provide the necessary fuel without charge.

254. Great care should be taken, in the preparation of vouchers for supplies to watchhouses, that the allowance

is not exceeded, and that the contract price (if any) is adhered to, and also that the proper form of voucher is used.

255. Vouchers for the conveyance of prisoners must in every case contain a certificate signed by a magistrate, stating the reason why they were not compelled to walk.

256. Vouchers for fees to medicial practitioners for evidence in cases of lunacy, must, in addition to the usual certificate for services performed, contain a certificate of the adjudicating justice or justices—that the examination was duly made, and evidence given in court. The fee for both must not exceed 21s. in each case.

257. The authorised fee for the visit of a medical man to prisoners or constables, in districts where no medical man is appointed to the Force, is in each case, for the first visit 5s., and for every visit after the first 2s. 6d., inclusive of medicines; for an operation, 21s.

258. In the case of the burial of paupers, or of bodies found drowned or dead in the bush, and buried at the public expense, it should be stated on the voucher if any inquest or magisterial inquiry has been held; in which case the expense is chargeable to the coroner's department, and should be transmitted to the Attorney-General. When there is no inquest or inquiry the expense will be defrayed by the Police Department.

259. The total expense of burials should in no case exceed £2 10s.

260. All other expenses not chargeable to the Police Department will be paid by the officers charged with the payment thereof, and to whom they should be sent direct.

261. Clothing, stationery, and stores of every description for police service, can only be obtained by a requisition on the printed form, with the columns thereof carefully filled up, which should be sent to the Commissioner, by whom it will be forwarded to the Colonial Secretary for approval; but if at any time the urgent want of any articles requires that they should be purchased in the district, this must only be done upon the authority of a

magistrate, and the voucher for the expense must bear a certificate explaining the reason why the articles were not obtained through the regular channel, signed by the magistrate authorising the expenditure.

262. Accounts for furniture and repairs should be sent to the Colonial Architect.

263. All vouchers, whether monthly or quarterly, should be sent to the Commissioner of Police at one and the same time, and accompanied by the printed letter of advice, stating the various items and showing the gross amount of the vouchers.

264. In order to facilitate the payment of vouchers, copies of authorities for special payments or appointments should be forwarded in support of the vouchers, for these services.

265. No cheque should be drawn until the amount thereof has been lodged in the Union Bank, Brisbane, by the Commissioner of Police, and duly advised. A statement of all cheques drawn monthly is to be forwarded with the usual acquittance.

266. Cheque books will be issued on application to the Commissioner of Police, and no cheque should be drawn except on the printed form supplied.

267. Butts of cheques, cancelled or otherwise, are to be transmitted to the Audit Office when the book is exhausted.

268. The allowance of clothing, arms, accoutrements, &c., is as follows, viz. :—

CLOTHING.

Sergeants and ordinary constables, per man—

Annually.

1 tunic	4 white covers for caps
1 ditto undress	2 glazed ditto ditto
1 pair dress trowsers	2 pair boots
2 pair undress ditto	4 shirts.
2 caps	

Biennially.	*Triennially.*
1 great coat.	1 oilskin cape.

269. The equipment for each constable consists of— 1 carbine with bayonet, muzzle stopper, scabbard, and frogs, 1 waistbelt with cartouche and cap pouches, 1 pistol, 10 rounds ball cartridge for carbines, 10 rounds ditto for pistols, 25 percussion caps, 1 pair handcuffs, 1 duty badge, 1 worm.

270. The allowance, in addition, for each station is— 1 nipple-wrench, 1 lock-cramp, 1 powder case and key, 2 spare nipples for every 5 carbines and pistols, 1 pistol cleaning rod, 1 carbine cleaning rod, 1 marching chain, leg irons.

271. Printed forms of all kinds are to be procured from the Government Printer upon the printed form of requisition.

DEFAULTER'S SHEET.

272. On a constable's misconducting himself, the particulars of the case, with his name, description, &c., are entered in a "defaulters' sheet," which must accompany him should he be transferred to any other district. On a constable who has never committed himself being transferred, a "defaulters' sheet," containing his name and description only, must be forwarded with him.

273. For the accuracy of these sheets the officers in charge of districts will be held responsible.

274. On the discharge or dismissal of any man from the Force, his "defaulters' sheet" must be forwarded to the office of the Commissioner, to be there filed for reference, and on the application, written or personal, of any one who has been discharged, a printed certificate of character will be made out in accordance with his sheet, signed by the Commissioner, and furnished to him, and no other certificates of character or service are to be given to parties leaving the Force. No certificates of character are given to those who have been dismissed.

CASES OF ILLNESS, ETC.

275. Any member of the Force consulting a medical man, without having first reported himself to the Sub-

Inspector, and obtained an order for medical advice, must pay the fee himself.

276. In ordinary cases of sickness a constable will be considered as on leave of absence, and paid in accordance with clause 11, page 6.

277. In cases of wounds or injuries received in the performance of his duty, a special report is to be made to the Commissioner; but should any constable be suffering from the effects of his own misconduct, his whole pay will be stopped during the time he is unfit for duty, and in such cases no order for medical attendance will be issued.

278. The medical practitioner must in all cases give a certificate of the cause of illness.

Confirmed, with the advice of the Executive Council, under my Hand, at Government House, Brisbane, this twelfth day of May, in the year of our Lord one thousand eight hundred and sixty-nine, and in the thirty-second year of Her Majesty's reign.

SAM. W. BLACKALL.

By His Excellency's Command,

ARTHUR HODGSON.

D

INSTRUCTIONS.

The following Instructions for the guidance of the Members of the Polic Force, in the performance of their duty, are published by the Commissioner of Police.

1. It is intended here to state such parts of the law relating to the office of constable, as may be sufficient for the general instruction of the Police Force.

2. Each individual will bear in mind the extreme importance of making himself perfectly acquainted with this subject, as it is necessary to enable him, with a due regard to his own safety, to act efficiently for the protection of the public.

3. It is especially necessary to take care that newly appointed constables do not form false notions of their duties and powers.

4. The powers of a constable, as will appear hereafter, are, when properly understood and duly executed, amply sufficient for their purpose. He is regarded as the legitimate peace officer of his district, and both by the Common Law and many Acts of the Legislature, he is invested with considerable powers, and has imposed on him the discharge of many important duties.

5. He is in many cases authorised and required, in the execution of his office, to arrest a party charged with or suspected to be guilty of some offence, to enter a house in pursuit of an offender, to quiet an affray, to search for stolen goods, to take possession of goods suspected to have been stolen.

6. It therefore becomes necessary that the constable should inform himself in what cases he ought so to interfere, and what legal powers he possesses to effect the object, in case he meets with resistance. To assist the Police Constables in the discharge of their duties, the following observations are prepared for their attentive perusal and study.

7. It will be first shewn for what offences of more ordinary occurrence a party may be arrested and detained in custody. With this object, offences may be divided into "Felonies" and "Misdemeanors."

8. Murder, rape, housebreaking, robbery, picking pockets, receiving stolen goods knowing them to have been stolen, assaulting any one with intent to rob, wounding, &c., with intent to do murder or some grievous bodily harm, setting fire to any church, house, or other building, are some of the principal felonies, besides a great many more too numerous to be inserted here.

9. Persons guilty of any of these offences are called felons.

10. Slighter offences, such as common assaults, affrays and riots, and various kinds of fraud, with numerous other offences, are called misdemeanors.

11. As it is more important to prevent and punish the commission of great crimes than of the lesser offences, the constable has a greater power in cases of felonies than in those of mere misdemeanors.

12. But the first duty of a constable is always to *prevent* the commission of crime.

13. A constable, by his appointment as such, has power to arrest, without warrant from a magistrate, a party whom from his situation and character the law judges to be likely to commit some felony, and persons found in the commission, charged with, or suspected of certain offences.

14. The constable may arrest any one whom he has just cause to suspect to be about to commit a felony; thus when a drunken person or a man in a violent passion threatens the life of another, the constable should interfere and arrest.

15. He should arrest any person having in his possession any picklock, key, crow, jack, bit, or other implement with intent feloniously to break into any dwelling-house, warehouse, coach-house, stable, or out-building; or any person armed with any gun, pistol, hanger, cutlass, bludgeon, or offensive weapon, or having upon him any instrument with intent to commit any felonious act.

16. Every person found in or upon any dwelling-house, warehouse, coach-house, out-house, or stable, or in any inclosed yard, garden, or area, or found in and on board any vessel when lying in any place within this colony for any unlawful purpose ; every suspected person or reputed thief frequenting any river, canal, or navigable stream, dock or basin, or any quay, wharf, or warehouse near or adjoining thereto, or any street, highway, or avenue leading thereto, or any place of public resort, or any avenue leading thereto, or any street, highway, or place adjacent, with intent to commit felony.

17. If any party threaten another with immediate personal violence or offer to strike, the constable should interfere and prevent a breach of the peace ; if one draw a weapon upon another, attempting to strike, the constable should take him into custody ; if persons are merely quarrelling or insulting each other, the constable has in general no right to take them into custody, but should be ready to prevent a breach of the peace.

18. In cases where an offence has not been actually committed, the constable must judge from the situation and behaviour of the party what his intention is ; in some cases no doubt can exist, as when the party is a notorious thief, or acting with those who are thieves, or when the party is seen to try peoples pockets in a crowd, or to attempt to break into a house, or to endeavor to take any property secretly from another ; the constable must not act hastily in case the intention is not clear, but content himself with watching closely the suspected party that he may discover his design.

19. The constable must arrest any one whom he sees in the act of committing a felony, or any one whom another positively charges with having committed a felony, or whom another suspects of having committed a felony, if the suspicion appear to the constable to be well founded, and provided the person so suspecting go with the constable.

20. Though no charge be made, yet if the constable suspect a person to have committed a felony, he should arrest him, and if he have reasonable grounds for his

suspicion he will be justified even though it should afterwards appear that no felony was in fact committed; but the constable must be very cautious in thus acting upon his own suspicions.

21. Generally if the arrest was made discreetly and fairly in pursuit of an offender, and not from any private motive or ill-will, the constable need not doubt that the law will protect him.

22. On the apprehension of any party for felony, if there is any reason to believe that any property connected with the felony will be found in the house or place in which the prisoner last resided, the arresting constable should in the presence of the party so arrested, search the premises he (the prisoner) has been occupying, and open any boxes, cases, or other receptacle of property belonging to the prisoner.

23. Every Member of the Police Force should do all in his power to prevent fraud upon the Revenue by evading the Acts for the regulation of Her Majesty's Customs, the Licensed Publicans, and Licensed Distilleries Acts, &c., for which purpose they will pay particular attention to the provisions of those Acts.

24. If after sunset, and before sunrise, the constable shall see any one carrying a bundle of goods which he suspects were stolen, he should stop and examine the person, and may detain him; but here also he should judge from circumstances, such as the appearance and manner of the party, his account of himself and the like, whether he really has stolen goods in his possession, before he actually takes him into custody.

25. He may also arrest any person whom he may find between sunset and sunrise lying or loitering in any highway, yard, or other place, and not giving a satisfactory account of himself.

26. The constable when justified in making an arrest, must use every exertion to effect it, and the law gives him abundant power for the purpose. If the felon or party accused of felony fly, he may be immediately followed wherever he goes, and if he takes refuge in a house the constable may break open the doors, if necessary to get

in, first stating who he is and his business; but the breaking open outer doors is so dangerous a proceeding, that the constable should never resort to it except in extreme cases, and when an immediate arrest is necessary.

27. There are some cases in which a constable may and ought to break into a house, although no felony has been committed, when the necessity of the case will not admit of delay, as when persons are fighting furiously in a house, or when a house has been entered by others with a felonious intent, and a felony will probably be committed unless the constable interferes, and there is no other means of entering. Except in such cases it is better, in general, that the constable should wait till he has a warrant from a Magistrate for the purpose.

28. If a Constable finds his exertions insufficient to effect the arrest, he ought to require all persons present to assist him, and they are bound to do so, on his stating that he is a constable and has lawful authority for what he is doing.

29. If a prisoner, on whatever charge lawfully taken, should escape, he may be retaken, and in immediate pursuit the constable may follow him into any place or any house, and if the escaped prisoner take refuge in a house, the doors may be broken open after demand of admission, and after notification by the constable of his office and object in coming.

30. In cases of misdemeanor the powers of the constable are not so extensive; he cannot generally arrest without a warrant, unless for offences committed within his own view, and when the arrest is specially authorised by law; and in executing the warrant and pursuing the offender he must be specially careful to act with the greatest forbearance.

31. In cases of actual breaches of the peace, as riots, affrays, assaults, and the like, committed within the view of the constable, he should immediately interfere (first giving public notice of his office, if he be not already known), separate the combatants, and prevent others from joining in the affray. If the riot, &c., be of a serious nature, or if the offenders do not immediately desist, he

should take them into custody, securing also the principal instigators of the tumult, and doing everything in his power to restore quiet.

32. A constable, in cases of assault which have not been committed in his presence or within his view, is not authorised to arrest or assist in arresting the party charged, nor is he to receive a person so charged into his custody, unless the party has been arrested by some other Constable who saw the assault committed. But if a person has been seriously cut or wounded, and gives into custody the party charged with having cut or wounded him, or in the case of any party being charged with committing any aggravated assault, which there is good reason to believe has been committed, and that by reason of the recent commission of the offence a warrant could not have been obtained for the apprehension of the offender, the constable is authorised to arrest the party, and keep him in safe custody until he can be brought before a magistrate.

33. A Justice of the Peace may by word of mouth command any constable or any other person to arrest another who shall be guilty of any felony or actual breach of the peace in his presence, and such command is a good warrant without writing, and must be obeyed accordingly.

34. A constable may arrest any one assaulting or opposing him in the execution of his duty, or any one aiding or assisting any person so to assault or to resist him.

35. If a person forcibly enter the house of another, the constable may, at the request of the owner, turn him out diaectly; if he entered peaceably, and the owner request the constable to turn him out, the constable should first request him to go out, and unless he do so, he should turn him out; in either case using no more force than necessary for that purpose.

36. When the offence has not yet been committed, but when a breach of the peace is likely to take place, as when persons are openly preparing to fight, the constable should desire them to desist, and if they do not do so, should take the parties concerned into custody; but if they fly

into a house, or are making preparations to fight within, the constable should enter to prevent them, and likewise take the parties into custody, and should the doors be closed, he may break them open if admission is refused, after giving notice of his office and his object in entering; but in all cases, if the parties are known, and no very violent breach of the peace has been committed, it is more advisable that they should be summoned before a Magistrate.

37. A constable may take into custody without warrant, all loose, idle, and disorderly persons whom he shall find disturbing the public peace, or whom he shall have good cause to suspect of having committed, or being about to commit any felony, misdemeanor, or breach of the peace.

38. A constable has power to apprehend and carry immediately, or as soon as possible, before a Justice of the Peace, any person whom he may find wilfully damaging any public building, wall, parapet, sluice, bridge, road, street, sewer, watercourse, or other public property; also any person who in his view commits any malicious injury to private property, and he should take charge of any person given into his custody who may have been arrested by the owner-of the property damaged, or by his servant or any person authorised by him.

39. After the arrest, the constable is in all cases to treat a prisoner properly, and impose only such restraint upon him as may be absolutely necessary for his safe custody.

40. The prisoner is to be taken as soon as convenient before the nearest Bench of Magistrates, who will dispose of the case, but he should in the first instance be taken to the watchhouse to have the charge regulary entered in the "Charge Book." · When the prisoner is brought to the justice, he still remains in custody of the constable until his discharge, committal, or conviction.

41. The constable is bound to follow the directions contained in a warrant, and to execute it with secrecy and despatch. The power given to him for the purpose of arresting, has been already shown. If the warrant cannot be executed immediately, it should be executed as soon as possible afterwards.

42. The constable must execute the warrrant himself, or when he calls in assistance, must be actually present. Upon all occasions he ought to state his authority, if it be not generally known, and should show his warrant when required to do so, but he should not part with the possession of the warrant, as it may be wanted afterwards for his own justification.

43. As it frequently happens that the warrant is in the hands of one constable, whilst another constable having undoubted information of such warrant, may find the accused person, or a person whom he has good ground to suppose to be such person, the latter ought in such cases to make the arrest, and if it be provable that a warrant has been issued, although it is not in his hands, he will be justified in his act, and will be entitled to the protection of the law. In such case he should communicate to the prisoner his information respecting the warrant.

44. A constable may enter a house to search for stolen goods, having received a search warrant from a magistrate for that purpose. He should, when it is possible to do so, execute it in the day time. If he finds the goods mentioned he is to take them to a magistrate, and when the warrant so directs, he must take the person also in whose possession they are found. To avoid mistakes the owner ought to attend at the search, to identify the goods, but this is not indispensably necessary in all cases.

45. In the following cases also, constables are empowered to arrest without warrant, but they are to be specially careful not to do so upon light grounds.

46. Any person found in the streets and public places in a state of intoxication, and behaving in a riotous and indecent manner, or incapable of taking care of himself.

47. Every common prostitute wandering in any street or public highway, or being in any place of public resort, who shall behave in a riotous or indecent manner.

48. Every person wandering abroad, or placing himself or herself in any public place to beg or gather alms, or causing, or procuring, or encouraging any child or children so to do, or endeavouring by the exposure of wounds or deformities to obtain alms, or endeavouring to

procure charitable contributions under any false or fraud-
ulent pretence.

49. Every person wilfully exposing to view in any public place, or who shall expose or cause to be exposed to
public view in the window, or other parts of any shop or
other building situate in any public place, any obscene
book, picture, or other indecent exhibition or· representation.

50. Every person wilfully or obscenely exposing his or
her person, in any street or road, or in the view thereof
or in any place of public resort.

51. Every person playing or betting at any unlawful
game.

. 52. Every person playing or betting in any street, road,
highway, or other open and public place, at or with any
table or instrument of gaming at any game or pretended
game of chance.

53. Any person who shall sing any obscene song or
ballad, or write or draw any indecent or obscene word,
figure, or representation, or use any obscene language in
any public place, or within the view or hearing of any
person passing therein.

54. Any person who shall use any threatening, abusive,
or insulting words or behaviour in any public place, with
intent to provoke a breach of the peace, or whereby a
breach of the peace may be occasioned.

55. Or any person who shall cruelly beat, ill-treat,
over-drive, abuse or torture, or cause or procure to be
cruelly beaten, ill-treated, over-driven, abused or tortured,
any animal.

56. In all these cases not only are constables empowered
to arrest without a Magistrate's warrant, but on fair and
sufficient grounds it is their duty to do so, and they are
also bound to receive into their custody any person found
committing any of these offences, who having been apprehended by another is delivered to them ; and any refusal
or wilful neglect to take such offender into their custody,
or to take or convey him or her before some Justice of
the Peace, will be a neglect of duty, and will render them
liable to the penalty attached to such neglect.

57. In cases where any soldier or member of any other public service shall appear intoxicated, it is advisable that the constable should communicate on the subject, through his superior officer, with the Officer under whose command the party is, and to refrain, except in cases of strong necessity, from taking him into custody.

58. There are many cases in which it is desirable that the Constable should only ascertain the name and residence of the party offending, and take the means of finding him afterwards. A report should be made to the superior officer, either immediately or when relieved, according to circumstances; and here it is to be remarked, that in any instance in which the power to arrest is not expressly stated, as in these and other instances to be hereafter mentioned, the constable is authorised to take into custody any person who within his view shall commit any such offences, and whose name and residence shall be unknown to such constable, and cannot be ascertained by him.

59. The constable should take notice if any houses, shops, or stores are kept open on Sundays for the purpose of trade, except for the dressing and selling of meat and victuals for such as cannot be otherwise provided, or chemists' shops, and should report the occupier of any such to the superior officer.

60. He must report any gaming on Sunday in any public billiard room or other place of amusement, taking care to ascertain the name of the owner or occupier of the premises.

61. He must also report the name of any publican or keeper of any house, shop, room, or place of public resort, wherein provisions, liquors, or refreshments of any kind shall be sold or consumed (whether the same shall be kept or retailed therein, or procured elsewhere), who shall wilfully or knowingly permit drunkenness or other disorderly conduct in such house, or; knowingly suffer any gambling whatsoever therein, or knowingly permit or suffer prostitutes or persons of notoriously bad character to meet together and remain therein.

62. Also any premises in which the cesspool has been allowed to overflow, or in such a filthy state from an accumulation of manure, dung, offal, soil, filth, coal ashes, or other matter, as to be a nuisance to the neighbors or injurious to the public health.

63. He should caution any person who may be about to bathe within that part of any river reserved to the public use for the supply of water, and report any person who shall so bathe, or who shall throw into the water any offal, carrion or other offensive thing, or obstruct any watercourse or public sewer, either by casting any filth or rubbish into the same, or in any other manner.

64. Protection is to be afforded to the Sheriff and Deputy Sheriffs in the execution of all writs from the superior courts, if in their written requisition they shall state that they have grounds to apprehend violence or opposition in the discharge of their duty.

65. In addition to the cases that have already been mentioned, there are numerous others under the various laws of the colony, in which constables may apprehend persons committing offences without warrant. The principal of these are under the Vagrant Act and the Towns and Country Police Act, both of which are included in a volume containing extracts of these and other Acts, and published for the use of the Police, and which should be carefully perused by every member of the Force. As to the manner in which the provisions of these Acts are carried into effect as already stated, much must of necessity be left to the individual discretion and judgment of members of the force.

66. The police are required to obey all magistrates in the execution of their judicial duties, by serving all legal processes, such as warrants, summonses, orders of court, &c.

67. The magistrates are not vested with any powers of interference with the interior executive arrangements of the Police Force ; but should they at any time suspect any felonious attempt upon life or property, of a nature so serious as to render it necessary for the public safety that they should act personally, then they are empowered

to call for the attendance of such of the police as they
may deem necessary ; and all constables so called upon
shall act under the magistrate's orders, so long as he is
personally present, and during the time necessary for the
suppression of such attempt.

SUMMONSES.

68. Summonses will be delivered to constables in duplicate, or with the original summons will be delivered a
copy. The constable should, in the first instance,
endeavor to serve the duplicate or copy, personally, that
is, deliver it into the possession of the individual to whom
it is addressed. Should it be a copy, he must produce
the original if required to do so by the party summoned.
In case the constable is unable from any cause to serve
the summons personally, it will be considered a legal and
effective service if it be left at the then or last usual place
of abode of the party named in the summons, or if it be
affixed to one of the doors or some other conspicuous
part of the outside of such abode ; although a summons
may be served either by day or night, constables will be
careful to execute this duty between sunrise and sunset as
much as possible, and in serving on the premises, they
are not to require admittance into the dwelling-house.
After service of a summons, the constable will make
before a magistrate an affidavit of the service (which must
be endorsed in the back of the original summons), as
follows :—

"Colony of Queensland, }
    To wit.   }
        "   of
police constable, maketh oath and saith that on the
        day of   instant, he this deponent did
(personally) serve the within-named   with a true
copy of this summons, by leaving the same (with   )
at his usual place of abode.
   "Sworn before me at   this
day of   18 ."

and will then return the original, without delay, to the
party from whom he originally received it.

CASES OF VIOLENT OR SUDDEN DEATH.

69. When the body of any deceased person is found by the police, or reported to them as having been found, it should be immediately removed to the nearest public house in the neighborhood, but where there are two or more public houses adjacent, the public-houses in such neighborhorhood are to be used alternately.

70. Every circumstance connected with the appearance of the body, the position in which it was found, and the probable length of time dead, should be noted; the body should then be carefully searched and the effects found thereon kept in the custody of the police and produced at the inquest.

71. The circumstances of the finding of a body, or of any case coming to the knowledge of the police where an inquest ought to be held, should be immediately reported to the Coroner, and to the senior officer of police in charge of the station.

72. Should the coroner be absent, or unable to attend, a communication to that effect should be forthwith made to the nearest magistrate, that he may hold an inquiry.

73. A constable is to remain in charge of the body until an inquest or inquiry has been held thereon.

74. On all occasions a report should be made to the coroner of the following cases :—Persons found drowned, persons found dead, persons killed by accident or otherwise, persons dying suddenly, prisoners dying in any of Her Majesty's Gaols or other places of confinement, suicides, and all other cases where death is suspected to have occurred from foul play, and a similar report, together with the result of the coroner's inquest or magisterial inquiry, should be made to the Commissioner of Police.

75. In cases of suicide, murder, &c., the instrument by which death had been induced, such as a knife, razor, pistol, &c., or bottle or paper which contained poison, should be carefully preserved by the police and produced at the inquest.

76. Immediately on any death occurring from any of the above causes, the police should endeavor to procure

evidence of identity of the deceased, and secure the
attendance at the coroner's inquest of the persons who
shall have found such body, or witnessed the circumstance
causing the death of the deceased, or who shall be able to
give any necessary information on the subject.

77. When the place is remote, and no coroner or police
or other magistrate is within a reasonable distance, they
should have the body examined by some medical gentle-
man if possible, but if not, the police must then make the
best examination they can themselves; the object being
in such cases to ascertain if death has been caused by
violence.

78. Should there be marks of violence on the body, it
is of importance to ascertain the instrument, if any, with
which the wounds have been inflicted.

79. If the wounds consist of a cut, the length, breadth,
and depth, should be ascertained as far as possible,
together with the exact position and appearances. If
firearms appear to have been used to cause death, it is
desirable to find the bullet or any other matter which
may have entered the body; but in all cases; before the
body or any weapon or other article which could in any
way be connected with the case is moved, or its position
altered, care should be taken that every particular is noted
in writing.

80. Every exertion should also be made to find the
particular weapon supposed to have been used, and if
found, its state when first seen by the police, should be
carefully noted, with all the other particulars.

81. The constable should then wait upon the nearest
magistrate and give his deposition, forwarding a copy
immediately to head quarters, with a full statement of all
particulars which may enable the Commissioner of Police
to judge if the matter has been properly inquired into by
the police.

82. Where a suspicion of felony attaches, the most
careful inquiry should be made of the names, both
christian and surname, of all persons who may be supposed
to know any circumstance connected with the death.
Above all things, every person without exception present

64

at the time of death should be examined before the coroner or magistrate.

83. The Police should not take upon themselves to bury the body, unless on the receipt of a certificate in the form for the purpose, from the coroner or justice of the peace.

84. In inquiries into violent deaths, the police officer in charge of the station at the time must consider himself as the person whose special duty it is to get up the case for the coroner or magistrate.

USE OF ARMS BY POLICE

85. The police are armed to enable them successfully ·to overcome opposition to lawful arrests,* and to protect themselves against armed interference in the execution of their duty. It is therefore of great importance that they should clearly understand under what circumstances they are justified in resorting to the use of the weapons with which they are entrusted.

86. It is only in the apprehension or detention of felons that a constable would be justified in proceeding to extremities, that is, when the constable is armed with a warrant for a felony, or when a felony is committed in his own view, or when he is in immediate or fresh pursuit of a person known to have committed a felony. Being satisfied on this point, to make the resort to firearms justifiable, it must be owing to some unavoidable necessity to which he must be reduced in the execution of his duty.

87. If a person having actually committed a felony will not suffer himself to be arrested, but stand on his own defence, or fly so that he cannot possibly be apprehended alive by those who pursue him, with or without a warrant from the magistrate, the constable in pursuit would be justified in using his weapon to secure him. The necessity for this proceeding (viz., that he cannot otherwise be taken) must be clearly apparent.

88. A police constable on duty at a gaol, or any other place in which prisoners are confined, is only justified in firing on any prisoner attempting to escape, who assaults or resists the constable endeavoring to retake or secure him, or on a prisoner committed for or convicted of

felony, who persists in flying from the gaol or other place of confinement, after reasonable efforts have been unsuccessfully made to capture him.

89. In all ordinary cases of police duty the baton is the weapon to which the constable should have recourse, and even the use of this should be avoided as much as possible, as good temper, with determination, will generally effect more than the use of violent measures.

90. The above remarks do not apply to cases of riot, &c., in which the police are called upon by the magistracy to act as an armed body, as on these occasions they will obey the orders of the magistrates, with whom the responsibility will rest.

www.ingramcontent.com/pod-product-compliance
Lightning Source LLC
Chambersburg PA
CBHW031451270326
41930CB00007B/940